S0-ARF-822

HOME REPAIR AND IMPROVEMENT

WORKING WITH WOOD

694
Wor   Working with wood.   21967

TIME®
LIFE
BOOKS

OTHER PUBLICATIONS:

DO IT YOURSELF
The Time-Life Complete Gardener
Home Repair and Improvement
The Art of Woodworking
Fix It Yourself

COOKING
Weight Watchers® Smart Choice Recipe Collection
Great Taste/Low Fat
Williams-Sonoma Kitchen Library

HISTORY
The American Story
Voices of the Civil War
The American Indians
Lost Civilizations
Mysteries of the Unknown
Time Frame
The Civil War
Cultural Atlas

TIME-LIFE KIDS
Library of First Questions and Answers
A Child's First Library of Learning
I Love Math
Nature Company Discoveries
Understanding Science & Nature

SCIENCE/NATURE
Voyage Through the Universe

For information on and a full description
of any of the Time-Life Books series listed above,
please call 1-800-621-7026 or write:

Reader Information
Time-Life Customer Service
P.O. Box C-32068
Richmond Virginia 23261-2068

HOME REPAIR AND IMPROVEMENT

WORKING
WITH WOOD

GLEN ROCK
PUBLIC LIBRARY

21967

BY THE EDITORS OF TIME-LIFE BOOKS, ALEXANDRIA, VIRGINIA

The Consultants

Jon Arno, a wood technologist residing in Michigan, where he works for a family lumber business, is known for his skills in furniture design and cabinetmaking. Mr. Arno has written extensively on the properties and use of wood and is the author of *The Woodworkers Visual Handbook* and a frequent contributor to *Fine Woodworking* magazine. He also conducts seminars on wood identification and early American furniture design.

CONTENTS

Wood and How to Cut It

Wood plays a central role in virtually any building or renovation project. Whether as lumber or as manufactured panels, it is readily available and relatively inexpensive. With the right tools and methods, cutting wood for most home projects is well within your reach.

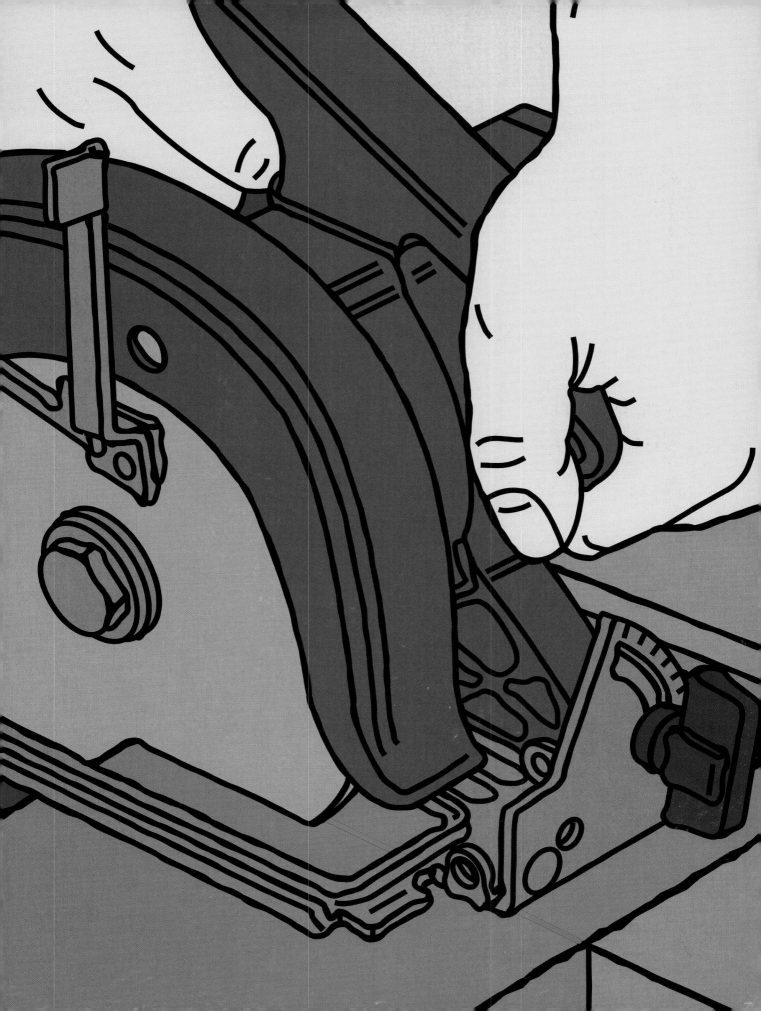

A Wood Primer

The quality of a carpenter's work depends as much on knowledge of wood as on skill with tools. Many problems can be prevented by choosing a wood product with its particular properties in mind.

Lumber: There are two classifications of lumber—hardwood and softwood. Hardwood is used primarily for flooring, fine interior trim, and furniture; softwood is the builder's choice for framing. Both types are graded by appearance and strength. Laminated veneer lumber (LVL) is a manufactured product that is sometimes used in place of regular lumber. LVL is lighter and stronger than lumber, and can be cut,

nailed, drilled, and shaped with common woodworking tools.

The size of a board is determined by its nominal rather than actual size. A board's nominal size is its width and thickness before it is planed smooth on all four sides at the sawmill. For example, a nominal 2-by-4 is actually $1\frac{1}{2}$ by $3\frac{1}{2}$ inches.

Manufactured Panels: Plywood, particleboard, hardboard, fiberboard, and other manufactured panels are ideal for covering large surfaces. They have consistent thickness and strength, and do not warp or shrink as much as lumber. Softwood plywood is the most common type, but hardboard is also available.

Moisture Content: As unseasoned or green lumber dries, its length remains virtually unchanged, but boards tend to shrink both in width and thickness. Wood that is not dried properly may warp as it shrinks. Though relatively unimportant in vertical framing members such as wall studs, warping in horizontal ones—top and sole plates, joists, and headers—can cause floors to sag and wallboard to crack. For the straightest lumber, buy boards stamped "KD" (kiln-dried) or "MC-15" (having a 15 percent moisture content). Store wood properly to keep it from absorbing moisture and warping further *(page 10)*.

 TOOLS

Circular saw
Electric drill
Spade bit ($1\frac{1}{8}$")
Masonry bit
Hammer
Carpenter's square
Carpenter's level

 **MATERIALS**

Heavy-duty plastic
  sheeting
Scrap lumber
Bricks
2 x 4s
Common nails
  (3", $3\frac{1}{2}$")
Masonry nails ($3\frac{1}{2}$")
Steel pipes (1")

 SAFETY TIPS

Put on safety goggles when nailing or when operating power tools

SELECTING WOOD

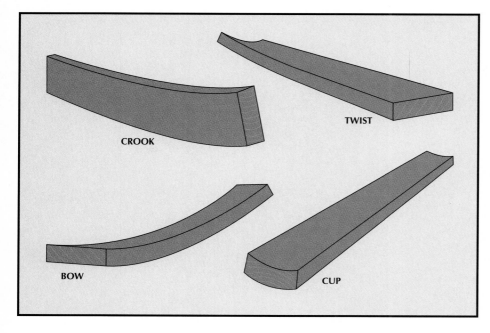

Four types of warping.
Check the straightness of a board by sighting along all four of its sides. A cup—a slight curve across the width of a board—does not seriously impair its strength or usefulness for general construction. A board with a crook (an end-to-end curve along an edge) or a bow (an end-to-end curve along a face) can be used horizontally with the convex side up, but do not use a board with either defect vertically in a load-bearing wall. Twisted boards are unstable and likely to distort more as they continue to dry; use them only if strength and straightness are unimportant.

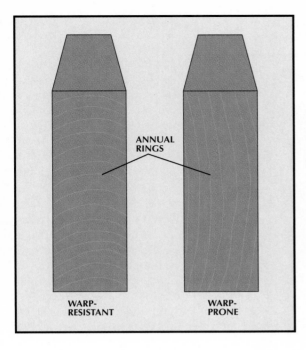

Good and bad ends.
Boards tend to shrink along their annual rings—the thin, concentric lines at the end of the board. Lumber with the rings parallel to the edges resists warping; boards with the rings paralleling the faces tend to warp as the wood moisture content changes. Do not use warp-prone boards where appearance or straightness is critical—in the rough framing for a door or window, for example.

GRADES OF LUMBER AND PLYWOOD

Softwood Lumber	Comments	Softwood Plywood	Comments
Appearance Grade		**Quality Designation**	
Select **B** and better	Highest quality; no knots; scarce	A	Knot-free
Select **C**	High quality; small defects	B	Tight knots
Select **D**	Good quality; defects can be concealed with paint	C	$1\frac{1}{2}$" knots
		D	$2\frac{1}{2}$" knots
Common		**Exposure Rating**	
Light Framing (*most widely used grades*)		Exterior	Fully waterproof bond; designed for permanent exposure to elements
Construction	Relatively few knots		
Standard	Minimum quality for most building needs		
Utility	Numerous knots; weak	Exposure 1	Fully waterproof bond; designed for long exposure during construction
Structural (*graded primarily by strength*)			
Select structural	Highest strength; few knots	Exposure 2	Moderately waterproof bond; designed for brief periods of exposure
No. 1	High strength; tight knots		
No. 2	High strength; many knots and blemishes		
No. 3	Low strength; rough appearance	Interior	Not suitable for any exposure to moisture; scarce
Studs (*specially designated as studs*)			
Stud	Suitable for all stud uses		
Utility stud	Good for nonload-bearing walls		

How wood is graded.
Lumber and manufactured panels are graded according to their quality and usage. Softwood lumber (*left-hand column*) is divided into two categories: appearance grade and common. Softwood plywood panels (*right-hand column*) are grouped by their appearance and by their ability to withstand exposure to weather and moisture. The face and back of a panel are often not of the same grade. A panel graded AC, for example, has an A-grade face with a C-grade back. Plywood may also have a stamp indicating its intended structural application such as flooring or sheathing.

STORING LUMBER

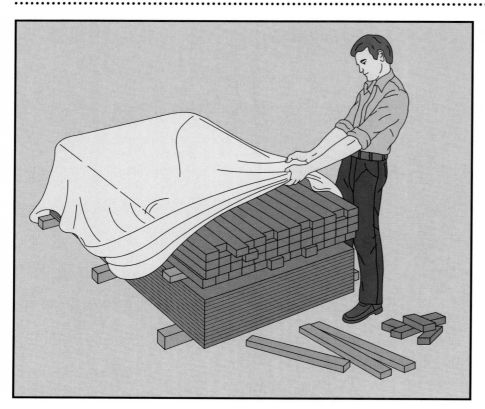

Stacking wood outdoors.
Arrange lumber or plywood in tight piles, raised 4 to 6 inches off the ground on wood scraps. Cover each stack with a sheet of heavy-duty plastic to shield the lumber from moisture *(left)*. Set wood scraps on top of the plastic and weigh them down with bricks. Place more scraps around the edges of the plastic to anchor the cover to the ground loosely enough to let air circulate under the pile and dissipate condensation from the underside of the plastic.

Check the pile periodically; if moisture has condensed under the plastic cover, loosen it to improve air circulation.

A rack for indoor storage.
The rack at right is ideal for storing lumber in a room with an unfinished ceiling. The two sections of the rack, spaced 2 feet apart, will support boards up to 4 feet long. For lumber up to 8 feet long, three sections are required; four sections are needed for longer boards.

◆ For each section, cut two 2-by-4 uprights 6 inches longer than the distance between the floor and the joists overhead. Drill $1\frac{1}{8}$-inch-diameter holes through the middle of the uprights' wide faces at 1-foot intervals.

◆ Measure the distance between the wall parallel to the joists and the outside face of the second joist. For each section, cut a 2-by-4 bottom plate $1\frac{1}{2}$ inches longer than this distance. Fasten an upright to each end of a bottom plate with $3\frac{1}{2}$-inch common nails.

◆ Set each bottom-plate assembly perpendicular to the wall, checking the angle with a carpenter's square. Fasten the plates to the floor with $3\frac{1}{2}$-inch masonry nails or a powder-actuated hammer.

◆ Plumb the uprights with a carpenter's level, and fasten them to the joists overhead with 3-inch common nails. If the joist along the wall is inset, nail wood scraps as spacers between the uprights and the joist.

◆ Slide 1-inch steel pipes through the holes in the uprights to support the lumber.

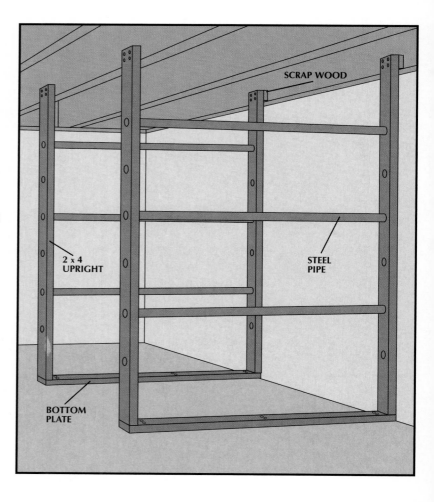

SCRAP WOOD

2 x 4 UPRIGHT

STEEL PIPE

BOTTOM PLATE

Wood Species	Characteristics
Softwood	
Cedar	Ideal for exterior uses because of its exceptional resistance to rot and termites. Easy to shape with tools, stable, and bonds well with glue and paint, but holds nails poorly.
Douglas-fir	Preferred for load-bearing members. Holds fasteners well, but does not take paint well. Tears badly when shaped with tools.
Fir, true	A common material for rough framing. Lightweight and fairly soft, but not very durable in exterior applications. Does not take paint or hold fasteners well.
Hemlock	Common for rough framing. Tends to warp and split; does not take paint or hold nails well.
Pine (except southern yellow)	Ideal for interior trim because it shapes and finishes well. Lightweight and about average in hardness and strength; dimensionally stable; holds nails, glues, and paint well.
Pine, southern yellow	Commonly used in stairways, girders, and rough framing. Stronger than most other softwoods. Holds fasteners well, but is difficult to shape with tools; tends to split when exposed to the weather, and does not hold paint well.
Redwood	Strong and resistant to decay. Ordinarily used for exposed surfaces only, because of its scarcity and high cost. Light, stable, and fairly rigid and hard; easy to shape with tools and holds glue and paint well.
Spruce	Used primarily for rough framing. Light, soft, and stable, with average strength. Easy to shape with tools, bonds well with glue, and holds fasteners well, but is difficult to paint.
Hardwood	
Birch	Used for fine interior trim, doors, and paneling. Heavy, hard, and strong; fairly easy to shape with tools, but tends to warp. Clear finishes are generally used.
Oak	Commonly used for flooring, doors, paneling, and interior trim. Heavy, hard, and very strong; difficult to shape with tools. Holds nails well, although it tends to split unless pilot holes are drilled first.
Panel Products	
Fiberboard	Used as sheathing for exterior walls. Light, soft, fairly flexible, and very weak. Easy to cut with tools and to glue, but does not hold nails and tends to shred when cut.
Hardboard	A good choice for siding, interior paneling, and floor underlayment. Fairly heavy and hard. Easy to shape with tools, though it shreds when cut; takes glue and paint well but does not hold fasteners well.
Particleboard	Used for underlayment and sheathing. Generally heavier and more rigid than hardboard, can be cut and glued easily, but is difficult to paint; may split when nails are driven into the edges.
Plywood	Uses include subflooring, wall and roof sheathing, exterior siding, interior paneling, and shelving. Heavy, fairly hard, and much stronger than other panel products. Easy to cut and shape with tools, and takes glue well; fasteners hold well when driven into the face, poorly when driven into the edge.

Comparing wood products. The chart above presents applications of various lumber species and wood products commonly used in house construction. It also describes their characteristics, such as weight, nail-holding ability, and the like. A wood that is said to be "stable" is one that does not respond to changes of humidity. The chart on pages 12 and 13 suggests the appropriate types, grades, and sizes of wood for a wide range of carpentry projects.

MATCHING MATERIALS TO THE JOB

Component	Material	Grade	Sizes	Comments
Carriage, stair	Softwood	Select structural	2 x 12	
Collar tie	Softwood	No. 2 or Construction	1 x 6, 2 x 4, 2 x 6	Size depends on roof load and rafter span.
Fascia board	Softwood	Select C or No. 1	1 x 6, 1 x 8	
Flooring	Hardwood	Clear or Select	$\frac{3}{4}$" thick, various lengths	Less expensive $\frac{3}{8}$" thick flooring may be available.
Furring strips	Softwood	Utility	1 x 2, 1 x 3	
Girder, built-up	Built-up softwood	No. 1, No. 2	2 x 10, 2 x 12	Straight lumber is essential; fasten boards side by side.
Girder, engineered beam	Laminated veneer lumber (LVL), Glulam	Industrial	$3\frac{1}{8}$" x 9" $3\frac{1}{8}$" x $10\frac{1}{2}$"	Beams can be ordered for almost any application; ask your dealer.
Header, plywood sandwich	Softwood	No. 1	2 x 4 (doubled) 2 x 6 (doubled) 2 x 8 (doubled) 2 x 10 (doubled)	Spans to 4 feet. Spans to 6 feet. Spans to 8 feet. Spans to 10 feet.
Header, engineered wood	LVL, Glulam	Industrial	$3\frac{1}{8}$" x $7\frac{1}{2}$" $3\frac{1}{2}$" x 12"	Spans to 9'3". Spans to 16'3".
Joist	Softwood	No. 1, No. 2	2 x 8 2 x 10 2 x 12	Spans to 11 feet. Spans to 14 feet. Spans to 16 feet.
Plate: top, sole, or sill	Softwood	No. 2	2 x 4, 2 x 6	Straight lumber is essential.
Post (for girder)	Softwood	No. 1	4 x 4, 4 x 6	Select pressure-treated lumber if the post will rest on concrete.
Rafter	Softwood	No. 1, No. 2	2 x 6 2 x 8 2 x 10	Spans to 9 feet. Spans to 15 feet. Spans to 20 feet. (Check with building code; may vary with pitch.)
Ridge beam	Softwood	No. 2	1" lumber	Select lumber at least 2" wider than rafters.
Riser, stair	Softwood	Select structural or No. 1	$\frac{3}{4}$" thick	Use No. 2 grade if stairs will be concealed by carpeting. Hardwood may be used to match the flooring.

Component	Material	Grade	Sizes	Comments
Sheathing Roof	Plywood	C-D	$\frac{3}{8}"$, $\frac{1}{2}"$, $\frac{5}{8}"$	Thickness depends on roof load; permissible rafter spacing stamped on sheet.
Wall	Plywood	C-D	$\frac{5}{16}"$, $\frac{3}{8}"$, $\frac{1}{2}"$	Thickness depends on stud spacing and wall material; use CDX type where weather is severe.
	Asphalt-impregnated fiberboard	Regular density	$\frac{1}{2}"$	Used primarily in new construction.
Shelving (rough)	Pine	Select B, C, or D or No. 2	1 x 8, 1 x 10, 1 x 12	Shelf supports must be 32 inches apart or less.
	Plywood	A-C, A-D, B-C	$\frac{1}{2}"$, $\frac{5}{8}"$, $\frac{3}{4}"$	Thickness depends on support spacing.
Studs	Softwood	Stud or Utility stud	2 x 4	Available only in lengths less than 10 feet. Utility studs are suitable only for nonload-bearing walls.
		No. 2	2 x 6	
Subflooring	Plywood	B-D, C-D plugged	$\frac{3}{4}"$	
Tread, stair	Softwood	Select structural or No. 1	$1\frac{1}{8}"$ thick	Choose No. 2 grade if stairs will be concealed by carpeting. Hardwood may be used to match the flooring.
Underlayment	Particleboard	1-B-1	$\frac{3}{8}"$ to $\frac{3}{4}"$	
	Hardboard	Underlayment grade	$\frac{1}{4}"$, $\frac{5}{16}"$, $\frac{3}{8}"$	
	Plywood	B-C plugged	$\frac{3}{8}"$ to $\frac{3}{4}"$	

Choosing a product for the job.

The first column of this chart lists the components of the frame and flooring of a house. The second specifies the appropriate material for each component. Where a softwood is indicated, choose a species that is available locally, inexpensive, and suitable for the application (chart, page 11). For hardwoods, oak is the most common choice. The third column indicates the minimum grade befitting the component in terms commonly used at most lumberyards; if different terms are used in your area, ask for the equivalent grades. The fourth column recommends board sizes for each component.

The specifications listed in the chart serve as a rule of thumb; any of the components may be subject to local building code requirements. Check the building code in your area and if you are unsure of any of the restrictions that apply in your case, consult an architect or a structural engineer.

Cutting Across the Grain

Any one of a number of hand and power saws can cut straight across the grain of wood, a process known as crosscutting. The most suitable saw for a particular project depends on the precision required, the number of cuts to be made, and the location of the job. Where the work must be done on site, a handsaw or a portable power saw is a good choice. When the work can be brought to the saw, crosscuts can be made on a radial-arm saw *(page 20)* or a table saw *(page 39)*.

Handsaws: The crosscut or all-purpose handsaw *(opposite)* offers several advantages over power saws.

Inexpensive, portable, and quiet, it requires no electricity to operate and is easier to get into awkward places. A blade that has 10 teeth, or points, per inch is best for general use; an 8-point saw makes quicker but rougher cuts.

Miter Boxes: For increased accuracy, use a backsaw and miter box *(page 16)*. Select a good-quality metal box that can accommodate boards up to 4 inches thick and 8 inches wide at any angle. When using the saw, anchor the miter box to a workbench, using bolts and wing nuts for easy removal.

Portable Power Saws: The most commonly employed power tool for crosscutting is the portable electric circular saw equipped with a multi-purpose or "combination" blade *(page 17)*. This saw makes quick work of trimming most lumber and, paired with a simple jig *(page 18)*, cuts with great precision. For home use, choose a model with a $1\frac{1}{2}$-horsepower motor and a $7\frac{1}{4}$-inch-diameter blade.

For a saw that will see frequent use, fit it with a carbide-tipped blade. Though more expensive than regular steel, carbide blades stay sharp at least 10 times longer.

 TOOLS

Combination square
Utility knife
Handsaw
Sawhorses
Miter box with
  backsaw
Circular saw
C-clamps

 MATERIALS

Plywood ($\frac{3}{4}$")
Stock for side
  brackets, guide,
  and stop
Paraffin
Wood screws
  (No. 8)

 SAFETY TIPS

Put on goggles when using a circular saw.

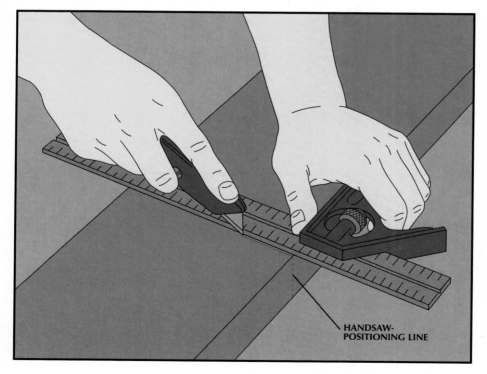

HANDSAW-POSITIONING LINE

Marking a crosscut.
Hold the handle of a combination square firmly against the edge of the board and mark along the blade. For rough cuts, use a pencil; for finer work, score the wood with a utility knife *(left)*—a scored line is more precise and helps prevent splintering as you cut the wood.

To help guide a handsaw, mark a second line at 90 degrees to the first across the edge of the board. This will help avoid unintentional beveling along the cut.

CROSSCUTTING WITH A HANDSAW

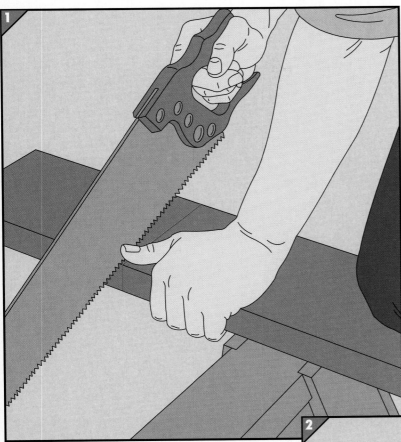

1. Starting the cut.

◆ Lay a board across two sawhorses, steady it with the knee opposite your cutting arm, and grip the saw handle so your index finger rests along the blade to help keep the saw in a straight line.

◆ With the blade just to the waste side of the cutting mark, set the end nearest the handle on the board edge at an angle of about 20 degrees.

◆ Holding the thumb of your free hand against the blade as a guide, draw the saw back toward you about one-half the blade's length, pressing lightly to cut into the wood *(left)*. Lift the blade clear of the wood and cut into it again in the same way. Repeat the process until the cut, or kerf, is at least as deep as the teeth, then draw the blade back and forth with short, smooth strokes, lengthening and deepening the kerf. As the saw sinks into the board, keep it aligned with the positioning line on the board's edge.

2. Cutting through the board.

◆ When the kerf is about 1 inch long, move your index finger to the handle.

◆ Gradually raise the angle of the saw to 45 degrees and lengthen the strokes so almost the full length of the saw—from about 3 inches from the tip nearly to the handle—is cutting the wood. Cut mainly on the forward stroke and apply moderate pressure *(right)*.

◆ When the cut is almost complete, reach over the top of the saw to hold the waste piece so it does not fall and splinter the wood.

If the saw binds in the wood, rub paraffin on the blade or drive a kerf splitter *(page 23)* into the kerf behind the blade. If the blade twists and binds as you attempt to correct a straying cut, either begin at a new location or reuse the old kerf and widen it until you reach uncut wood.

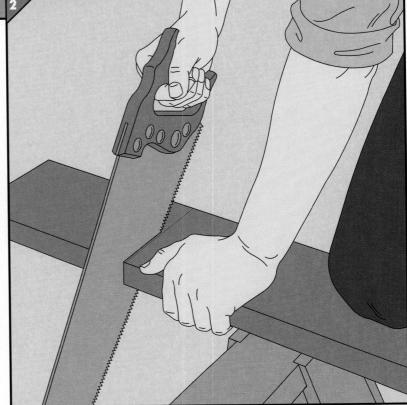

A MITER BOX FOR PRECISION

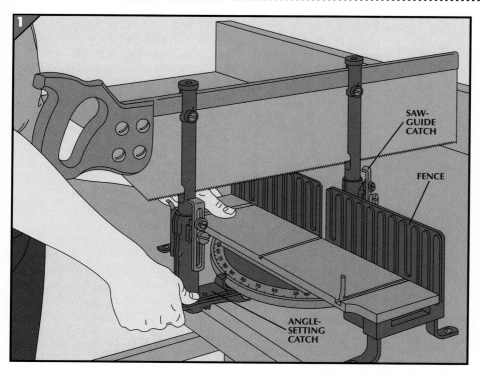

SAW-GUIDE CATCH

FENCE

ANGLE-SETTING CATCH

1. Setting the angle.
◆ With the blade raised, release the catch on the miter box's angle-setting device and move the pointer to the desired mark—for a crosscut, 90 degrees *(left)*.
◆ Position the board on the base against the fence with the cutting mark aligned under the saw blade. Release the front and back saw-guide catches and, holding the blade just above the board, shift the board as necessary to position the cutting mark directly under the blade.

2. Making the cut.
◆ Adjust the miter-box clamps to steady the board against the frame. If the board is too short to reach one or both clamps, hold it with a thumb.
◆ Begin the cut with a series of backward strokes, holding the saw level to cut the entire upper surface of the wood. Then, applying pressure on the forward strokes, cut the rest of the way through the board with long, smooth strokes that fall just short of pulling the blade from the rear guide or running the handle into the front guide *(right)*.

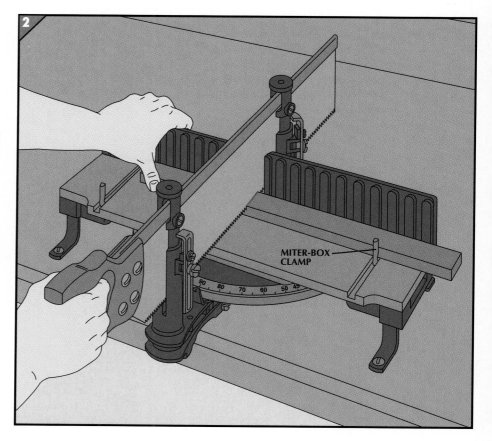

MITER-BOX CLAMP

FREEHAND CUTS WITH A CIRCULAR SAW

1. Aligning the saw.
◆ Lay the board across two sawhorses and steady it with your knee.
◆ Place the saw's base plate on the board with the blade $\frac{1}{2}$ inch back from the edge. Set the saw's cutting depth so one entire blade tooth will extend below the bottom of the board. With the notch in the base plate as a guide, align the blade on the waste side of the cutting line *(right)*.

The guide in the base plate is generally an effective device for aligning a straight cut, but after changing or sharpening the blade, the guide may not line up precisely with the teeth of the blade. Many experienced carpenters ignore the guide and align the teeth along the cutting line.

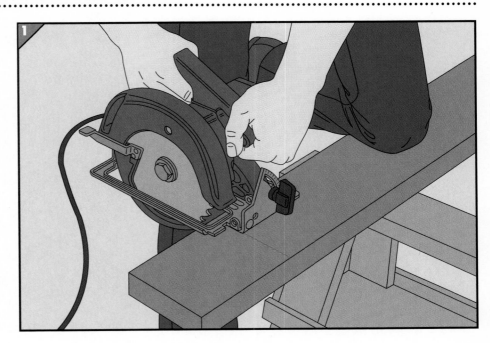

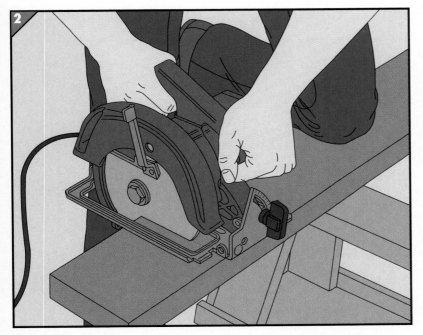

2. Making the cut.
◆ Start the saw and ease the blade into the board, keeping it on the line. Allow the blade to work its way through the wood—do not force it *(above)*.
◆ If the blade strays off course, release the switch, pull the saw out of the kerf and start the cut again, carefully following the marked line. If the blade binds in the kerf, return to the start of the kerf, and cut slowly into it again. If the weight of the waste end of the board is causing the blade to bind, support the waste with a sawhorse.
◆ Near the end of the cut, slow the saw's forward motion, then cut quickly through the remainder of the board with a swift stroke. Release the switch and check that the blade guard has returned to its closed position.

Circular Saw Safety

✔ Follow all the manufacturer's instructions.
✔ Use only a double-insulated or grounded saw, and plug the tool into a grounded outlet.
✔ Keep children and pets out of the work area, and clean up frequently to avoid clutter.
✔ Do not wear loose clothing, a necktie, or jewelry.
✔ Put on goggles when cutting.
✔ Do not stand directly behind the saw; if the blade binds, the saw may kick back at you.
✔ Never place your fingers beneath a board being cut.
✔ Before setting the saw down, make sure that the blade guard is closed.
✔ Never carry the saw with your finger on the trigger.
✔ Unplug the saw when adjusting the saw's settings or changing the blade.
✔ Clean built-up resin from the blade with kerosene or a commercial solvent.

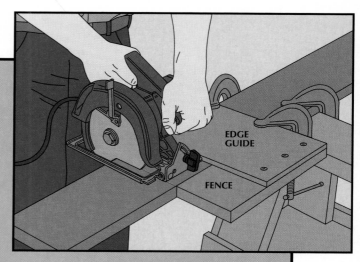

TRICKS OF THE TRADE

A Simple Crosscutting Jig

An easy-to-build jig can help you make crosscuts with a circular saw. Cut a 6- by 10-inch piece of $\frac{1}{2}$-inch plywood to make the edge guide, and a 4- by 10-inch piece of $\frac{3}{4}$-inch plywood for the fence. Screw the pieces together in an L shape with 1-inch No. 8 wood screws, using a combination square to keep them perpendicular.

To crosscut with the jig, mark a cutting line on the board, then lay it across a pair of sawhorses. Set the jig against the board and clamp the two together, then clamp the board to the sawhorse. Make the cut with the saw's base plate pressed against the edge guide

(above), cutting across the end of the fence if it projects beyond the cutting line. For subsequent cuts, align the end of the fence with the cutting mark on each board.

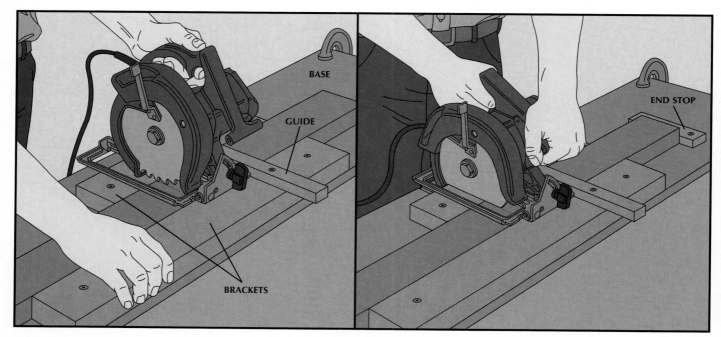

A jig for repeat cuts.

◆ Set the first board to be cut on a $\frac{3}{4}$-inch-plywood base and bracket it with two scrap boards of the same thickness. Fasten the brackets to the base with No. 8 wood screws and secure a strip of wood as a guide across the top of the scraps at a right angle to the board.

◆ Elevate the saw blade fully and set the saw on the brackets and against the guide *(above, left).* Slide the board between the brackets and align the blade on the waste side of the cutting line. Screw a block of wood to

the base at the far end of the board to serve as a stop.

◆ Set the blade depth to slightly more than the board's thickness. Run the saw along the guide to cut through the board and the side brackets *(above, right).* Cut more boards to the same length by slipping them one at a time into the jig and against the stop.

To cut several pieces to the same length simultaneously, widen the jig to hold the pieces side by side and make a long end stop parallel to the guide.

The Radial-Arm Saw

The radial-arm saw is an ideal all-purpose stationary saw if you have limited shop space or a tight budget. Well suited for crosscutting many boards to the same length and angle *(page 21)*, it can also rip stock—cut it along the grain—to any width up to about 24 inches.

Adjustment and Setup: Many of the radial-arm saw's parts can be moved *(below)*, giving the machine versatility, but each of these parts must be properly adjusted for the saw to cut accurately. Check and fine-tune the adjustments periodically.

Blades and Accessories: For crosscutting, you can use a standard multi-purpose steel blade or a longer-lasting carbide-tipped model. In either case, ask for a blade designed for a radial arm saw with teeth having a hook angle of 5 degrees or less; this should be specified on the blade manufacturer's label. For fine cutting, such as for trim, mount a planer blade.

Most radial-arm saws come equipped with a warp-resistant particleboard table top. To protect this surface, fasten a disposable sheet of $\frac{1}{4}$-inch tempered hardboard to it with countersunk wood screws; locate the fasteners so they won't get in the way of the blade at any of its settings. When cutting long stock, also position an extension table at each side of the saw.

 TOOLS

Hammer

 **MATERIALS**

1 x 4
Common nails (2")

 SAFETY TIPS

Wear goggles when driving nails or when operating a power tool.

ANATOMY OF A VERSATILE SAW

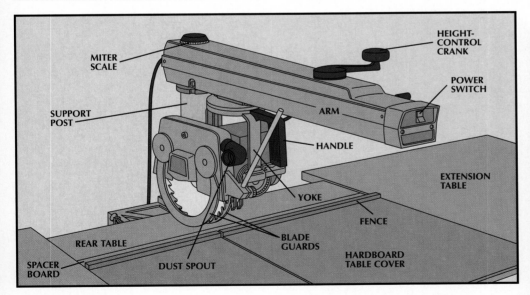

A versatile cutter.

This saw's motor is suspended above the table in a yoke that permits it to tilt 100 degrees right or left. The yoke can also rotate more than 360 degrees in its swivel mount, which rides in a track beneath the arm. The arm can move up and down as well as 105 degrees to both right and left. A miter scale shows the angle of the arm in relation to the replaceable fence. For crosscutting, the saw is pulled forward, cutting through the fence and board, and into the surface of the hardboard table cover. The blade is shielded by guards, and a dust spout directs sawdust to the side. Other locks and safety features are provided for rip cuts *(pages 24-27)* and angle cuts *(page 32)*.

Radial-Arm Saw Safety

✔ Plan cuts before starting the motor; concentrate on the cut at hand, and turn the motor off as soon as it is done.
✔ Hold the board being cut firmly against the fence, keeping your hand well away from the blade. Never place your fingers on the back of the fence.
✔ Pull the blade forward only until its bottom edge emerges from the wood; then push the saw immediately to its rear position and turn it off.
✔ Clean off any built-up resin from the blade with kerosene or a commercial solvent.

21967

BASIC CROSSCUTTING

1. Setting up the cut.

◆ With the motor off and in its rear position behind the fence, set the miter scale on the arm at 0 degrees and the blade $\frac{1}{8}$ inch below the level of the hardboard table cover.

◆ Place the board against the fence. With the blade almost touching the board, position the board so the blade is just to the waste side of the cutting line *(right)*.

◆ With the fingers of your left hand on the board at least 6 inches from the cutting line, press the board against the fence with your thumb.

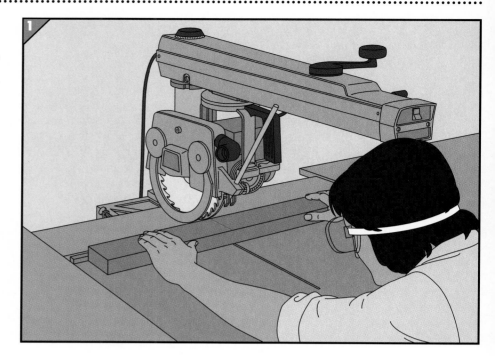

2. Making the cut.

◆ Still holding the board against the fence, start the motor and, with a firm grip on the handle, pull the blade into the board *(left)*. If the blade tends to climb over the board and bind there, lock your elbow by straightening your arm. If you cannot keep the blade from climbing over the board, shut off the saw at once, and start the cut again, this time in two passes. For the first pass, raise the blade to cut only about halfway through the board's thickness; for the second pass, return the saw to the initial cutting height.

◆ When the bottom of the blade emerges from the front edge of the board *(inset)*, return the saw to its rear position and shut it off.

⚠ **CAUTION** *Avoid pulling the blade completely through the cut board—the saw teeth spinning upward at the rear may catch the waste piece and hurl it over the fence.*

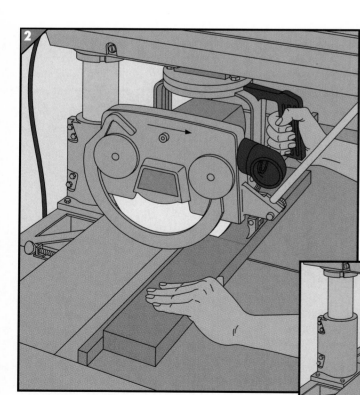

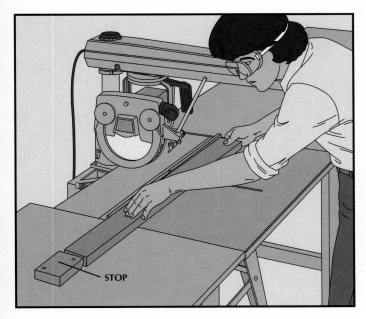

STOP

End stops for repeat cuts.

A 1-by-4 stop fastened to an extension table beside the saw will let you crosscut a series of long boards to the same length.

◆ Bevel *(page 32)* the end of the stop that will contact the boards to prevent accumulating sawdust from creating a gap between the stop and the boards.

◆ To set up the stop, position the first board against the fence with the cutting line aligned with the blade *(opposite, Step 1)*. Butt the stop against the board, then nail it to the table with 2-inch common nails.

◆ To use the stop, slide the workpiece along the fence until it contacts the stop *(left)*, then make the cut.

TRICKS OF THE TRADE

A Simple Clamp-Stop

You can set up an end stop for cutting short boards by fastening a handscrew clamp to the fence *(right)*. Leave a gap between the clamp and the table to prevent sawdust from accumulating between the work and the stop.

Cutting thick lumber.

You can follow this technique to saw wood up to twice as thick as the distance between the bottom of the motor and the blade teeth.

◆ Raise the blade until the motor clears the board, then make the cut across the top of the board.

◆ Turn the board over, align the kerf with the blade *(left)*, and pull the saw to cut the board in two.

Cutting a board lengthwise, a process called ripping, is necessary for certain jobs such as fashioning stair treads and risers, odd-size jambs for thick walls, or new studs to match old, full-size lumber.

Handsaws: Ripping is seldom done with a handsaw. Because the blade tends to follow the grain, holding a straight line is difficult. But for hard-to-reach spots or when a board is too small to be cut safely with a power saw, a handsaw is the only alternative; however, if the cut edge will be exposed, you will need to plane the wood smooth afterward. When marking such pieces for a cut, allow an extra $\frac{1}{16}$ inch for the planing. Use a $5\frac{1}{2}$- to 6-point ripsaw to make the cut.

Circular Saws: Equipped with a carbide-tipped combination blade, a portable circular saw will easily rip boards; you can obtain smoother edges with a hollow-ground planer blade. A circular saw is not very precise when used freehand; for more accuracy, use a rip guide *(opposite)* or a panel-cutting guide *(pages 33-34)*.

Stationary Saws: A radial-arm saw *(pages 24-27)*—adjusted to the "in-rip" position for narrow boards and the "out-rip" position for wide pieces—or a table saw *(pages 39-40)* combines speed and precision. With either saw, consider buying a rip blade—its chisel-shaped teeth with deep recesses between them excel at cutting with the grain. A carbide-tipped blade is a worthwhile investment if you plan to do a great deal of ripping.

To cut long pieces, position an extension table or support on each side of the saw.

 TOOLS

Combination square
Marking gauge
Vise
Ripsaw
Sawhorses
C-clamps

Circular saw with guide arm
Kerf splitter
Radial-arm saw
Tape measure
Push stick

 **MATERIALS**

Scrap wood

 **SAFETY TIPS**

Goggles protect your eyes when you are operating a power saw.

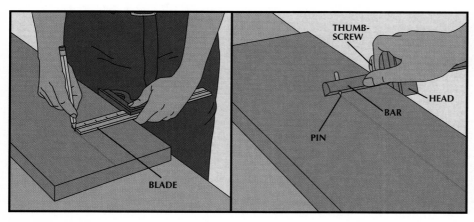

Marking a rip cut.
You can accurately mark boards for rip cuts using either a combination square or a marking gauge. With a combination square, extend the blade to the desired cutting width and lock it. Holding a pencil against the end of the blade, slide the square along the edge of the board *(above, left)*.

To use a marking gauge, set the distance between the head and the spur and tighten the thumbscrew. Holding the head against the board, roll it forward until the pin barely touches the board, then push the gauge along the board *(above, right)* to score the cutting line in the wood.

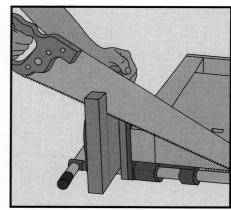

Ripping a short board by hand.
◆ Secure the board vertically in a vise so the cutting line is outside the jaws. With a ripsaw, start the cut as you would for a crosscut *(page 15)*.
◆ Once the teeth are completely in the kerf, steady the board with your free hand *(above)*. To minimize tearout as you near the end of the cut, straighten the blade so the teeth are nearly parallel to the end of the board.

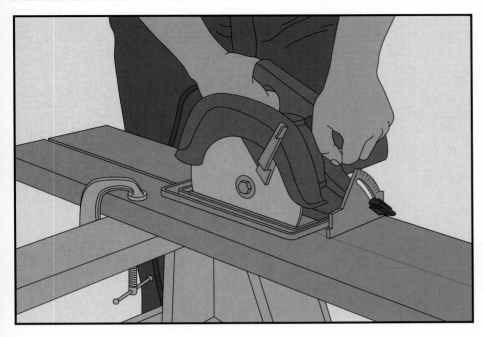

Cutting freehand.

◆ Clamp the board to two sawhorses and set the saw's blade depth $\frac{1}{4}$ inch more than the thickness of the board.

◆ Set the saw on the end of the board and align the base-plate guide mark or the blade itself with the cutting line.

◆ Start the saw and ease the blade into the board. Guide the saw with both hands (left), keeping the blade in line with the cutting mark. If the motor labors, push the saw more slowly. If the cut strays off line, angle the saw slightly toward the line, then straighten it when the cut gets back on line. If the blade binds, turn off the saw and insert a kerf splitter (below) into the cut near the blade.

TRICKS OF THE TRADE

A Kerf Splitter

Designed to keep the kerf open behind a binding blade, kerf splitters are available commercially, but you can easily make your own. Cut a $1\frac{3}{4}$- by $3\frac{1}{2}$-inch piece of $\frac{1}{8}$-inch hardboard for the splitter and a 1- by 3-inch $\frac{3}{4}$-inch plywood rectangle for each shoulder. Cut off the front corners of the shoulders for easier handling. Glue the three pieces together (below). To free a binding blade, turn off the saw and insert the splitter into the cut about 6 inches behind the blade. Pull the saw back slightly, then continue the cut. Move the splitter along the cut if necessary.

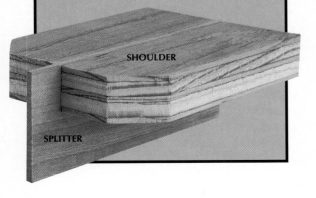

SHOULDER

SPLITTER

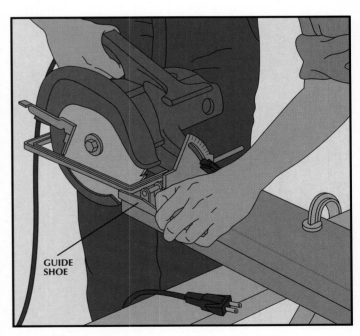

GUIDE SHOE

A built-in rip fence.

Some circular saws come with a guide designed to improve the accuracy of rip cuts.

◆ With the saw unplugged, set the front of the base plate flat on the board and align the blade with the cutting line.

◆ Slide the guide's arm through its holder on the saw's base plate so the shoe sits against the edge of the board (above). Tighten the arm in place.

◆ Saw the board as for a freehand cut, maintaining a gentle sideways pressure on the saw to keep the guide shoe tight against the edge of the board.

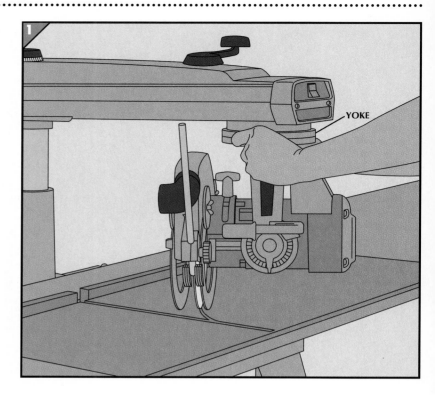

1. Setting the in-rip position.

◆ With the motor off and the blade depth set $\frac{1}{8}$ inch below the table top, pull the yoke forward to the end of the arm and fix it in position by tightening the rip lock.

◆ Start the motor, grip the saw handle with your left hand, and release the yoke lock with your right. Pivot the motor slowly clockwise with both hands, cutting a shallow quarter-circle into the hardboard table cover *(right)*. Once the motor completes the quarter-circle, a cog in the yoke mechanism will lock the blade parallel to the fence in the in-rip position, with the motor away from the fence. Leave the motor on and proceed immediately to Step 2.

YOKE

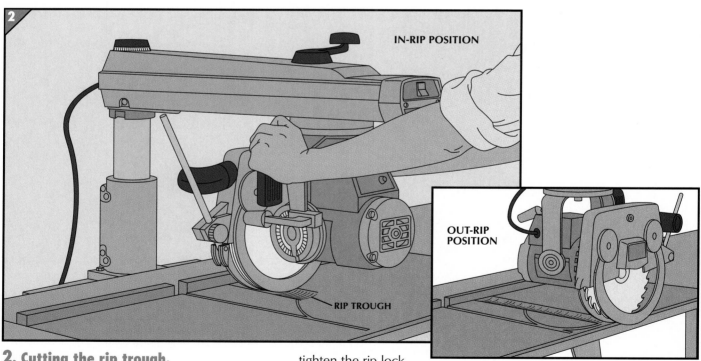

IN-RIP POSITION

OUT-RIP POSITION

RIP TROUGH

2. Cutting the rip trough.

◆ Release the rip lock and, using both hands, slowly push the saw toward the back of the table, cutting a shallow trough in the table cover *(above)*.

◆ When the blade guard reaches the fence, pull the yoke back to the end of the arm and

tighten the rip lock.

◆ Release the yoke lock and pivot the yoke 180 degrees to the out-rip position—with the motor facing the fence.

◆ Loosen the rip lock and slowly push the saw back, continuing the trough *(inset)*.

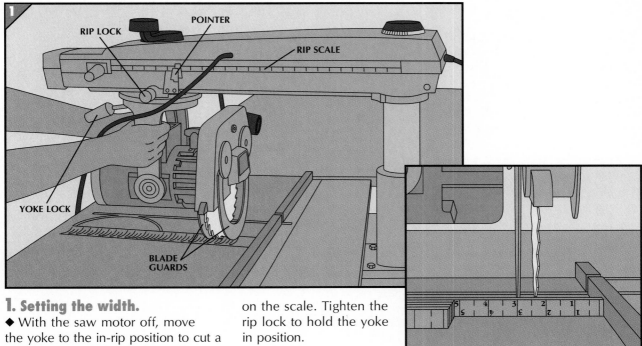

1. Setting the width.

◆ With the saw motor off, move the yoke to the in-rip position to cut a width less than 8 inches *(above)*; for wider cuts, move the yoke to the out-rip position. Engage the yoke lock.

◆ To set the width of cut, lift the blade guard closest to the fence and push the yoke along the arm until the pointer indicates the desired width on the scale. Tighten the rip lock to hold the yoke in position.

For a more accurate measurement, check that the blade is the desired distance from the fence *(inset)*; or, set the workpiece against the fence and align the blade with the cutting line.

2. Adjusting the blade guard.

◆ Place the board (or a wood scrap of the same thickness) beside the blade and loosen the wing nut that locks the blade guard to the motor.

◆ Rotate the guard until the spring clip on its nose applies pressure against the board *(right)*, then tighten the wing nut, locking the guard in place.

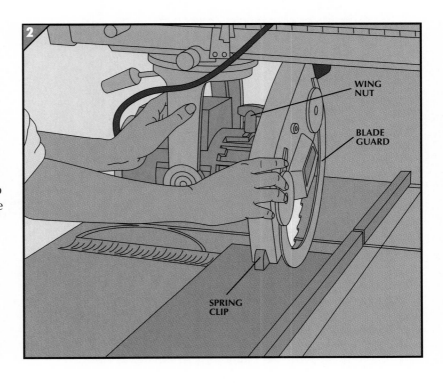

3. Setting antikickback fingers.

◆ Place the board just beside the antikickback fingers at the back of the guard.

◆ Loosen the clamp that secures the rod holding the fingers. Lower the rod until the fingers dangle $\frac{1}{8}$ inch below the top of the board, then tighten the clamp (right).

◆ To test the fingers, slide a board under them from the blade side, then reverse direction back toward the blade (inset). If the fingers do not bite into the top of the board and prevent it from moving back, lower the rod and retest.

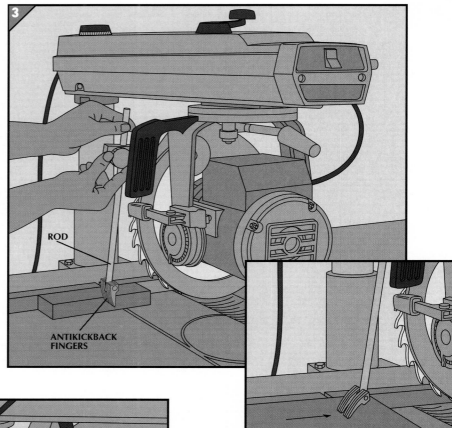

ROD

ANTIKICKBACK
FINGERS

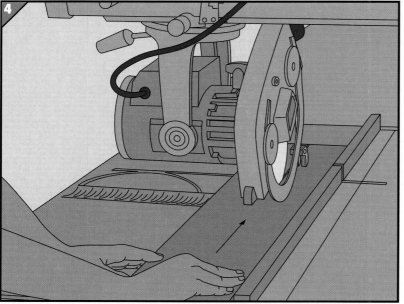

4. Starting the cut.

◆ Set the board flat on the table and against the fence. Turn on the saw and place your hands on the board about 18 inches behind the blade, with one hand next to the fence and the other on the opposite edge (above).

◆ Slowly push the board into the blade with the hand next to the fence; use your other hand to press the board gently down and against the fence.

◆ When your hands are about 6 inches from the blade, move them back along the board, without losing contact with it, and continue the cut. If the blade binds, shut off the saw and open the cut with a kerf splitter (page 23), then pull the workpiece back slightly and continue the cut.

◆ When your hands are on the end of the board and 6 inches from the blade, go to Step 5.

Safe Ripping with a Radial-Arm Saw

When you rip with a radial-arm saw, the blade may lift the workpiece off the table and throw it back at you. In addition to the safety tips on page 19, observe the following precautions

✔ Keep the workpiece pressed against the table, using a spring clip (page 25, Step 2) or hold-down wheels (opposite).

✔ Set the antikickback fingers (above, Step 3).

✔ Feed the board from the right of the saw when in-ripping, and from the left when out-ripping.

✔ Stand beside, not behind, the board.

5. Completing the cut.

If the distance between the blade and the fence exceeds 6 inches, you can complete the cut with the hand near the fence. Position your hand at the end of the board, thumb tucked under your palm.

Where the distance is 1 to 6 inches, advance the board with a push stick. Place the stick's notch on the end of the board, centered between the blade and the fence, and push the board through the blade *(right)*.

With a distance of less than 1 inch, set a wood scrap about 16 inches long and 3 inches wide at the end of the board and against the fence. Push the scrap to feed the workpiece forward until it is free of the blade *(inset)*, then turn off the saw and slide out the scrap.

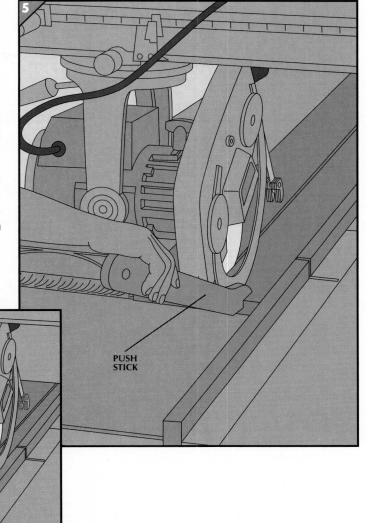

PUSH
STICK

SCRAP
WOOD

TRICKS OF THE TRADE

Hold-Down Wheels to Prevent Kickback

With rubber wheels that ride along the top of the workpiece, this hold-down device presses a board against the saw table. The mechanism has pins which are inserted into holes drilled into the fence at a slight angle so the wheels also push the board against the fence. Designed to rotate in one direction only, the wheels lock in the event of kickback.

Three types of angled cuts are required in carpentry. A miter cut slants across the face of a board, while a bevel cut slants across an edge between opposite faces. A compound cut combines the two, yielding a board that is both mitered across its face and beveled across its edge.

Saw and Guides: The same saws used for square cuts will also make angled ones. Aided by simple wooden guides, both handsaws and circular saws will cut accurately *(opposite and page 31)*. For even greater precision with trim such as casings, baseboards, and molding, use a miter box and backsaw *(page 30)*. Radial-arm saws, table saws, and power miter saws also produce fast and accurate angled cuts *(page 32)*.

Scale Error: The angle scales on power tools are rarely accurate. While the error generally is small —around 1 percent—it can sometimes spoil a visible joint. You will need to compensate slightly to cut precise angles.

The most accurate way to copy an angle and transfer it to a board or a saw is with a T-bevel *(below)*. For fine work, make a test cut on scrap wood, check the angle, and readjust the saw, if necessary.

 **TOOLS**

T-bevel	Miter box with
Sawhorses	backsaw
Handsaw	Circular saw
C-clamps	Radial-arm saw
Hammer	

 MATERIALS

Scrap wood
Common nails

SAFETY TIPS

Put on goggles when driving nails or operating a power tool.

COPYING AN ANGLE WITH A T-BEVEL

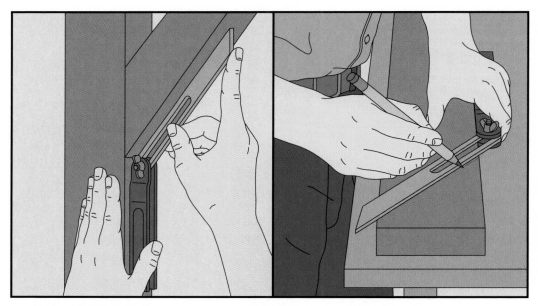

Transferring an angle.
◆ Loosen the wing nut on the T-bevel and extend the blade.
◆ Fit the tool into the angle to be transferred so the blade and handle are both flush against the adjoining surfaces *(above, left)*, then tighten the wing nut to lock the blade in place.
◆ To mark the angle on a board, hold the handle of the T-bevel against the edge so the blade crosses the face, then run a pencil along the blade *(above, right)*.

MITERING ROUGH LUMBER

Cutting an angle with a handsaw.
◆ Clamp a scrap 2-by-4 across the board so that it lines up with the cutting line.
◆ Start the cut as for a crosscut *(page 15)*, resting the side of the saw blade against the guide *(right)*. After establishing the kerf, remove the saw from the board and check that you are following the cutting line. If not, reposition the guide and restart the cut.

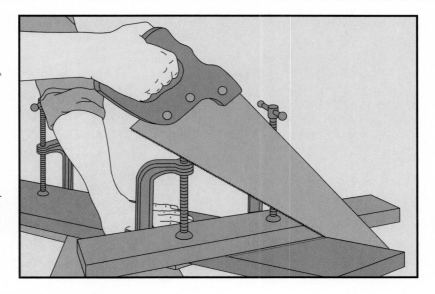

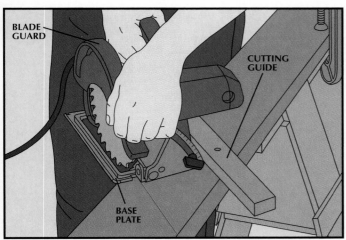

Mitering with a circular saw.
◆ Align the saw blade on the waste side of the cutting line and mark the position of the left-hand edge of the base plate on the board. Nail or clamp a scrap 2-by-4 at the mark parallel with the cutting mark.
◆ With the base plate against the guide, start the cut. Depending on the angle, the blade guard may not automatically retract; in this case, turn off the power, lift the blade guard, and hold it up as you begin the cut *(left)*. Release the guard after it clears the edge of the board. If the blade strays from the cutting line during the cut, start it over—do not attempt to force the saw back on course.

TRICKS OF THE TRADE

A Jig for Miters and Crosscuts

The jig shown at right will allow you to make either 45-degree miter cuts or 90-degree crosscuts. Fashion the jig from $\frac{3}{4}$-inch plywood, cutting it 16 by 16 by $22\frac{5}{8}$ inches to form a triangle with one 90-degree corner and two 45-degree ones. Use scrap wood to make two $\frac{3}{4}$- by $\frac{3}{4}$-inch fences, attaching them to opposite faces along one of the short edges with 2-inch No. 6 wood screws.

To cut a miter with the jig and a circular saw, clamp the jig to the board with the fences tight against the edge of the board.

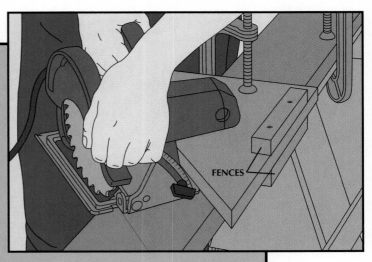

Run the saw along the jig as you make the cut *(above)*. To make a crosscut, use the square side of the jig as your guide.

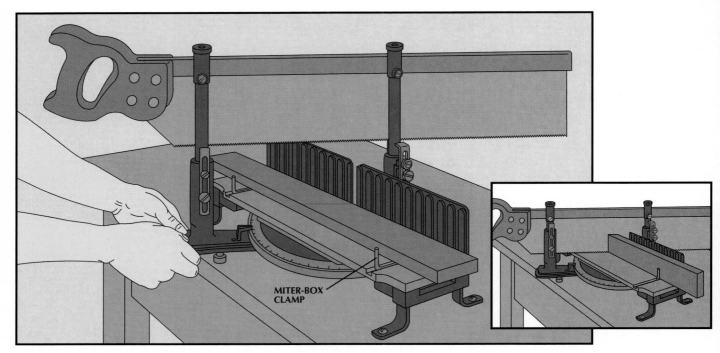

Making a miter or bevel cut.
◆ For a miter cut, place the board flat side down in the miter box.
◆ Set the saw to the desired angle *(above)*.
◆ Position the board so the saw is aligned just to the waste side of the mark; if neces-sary, reset the angle. Secure the board with the miter-box clamps or C-clamps.
◆ Lower the saw and make the cut.

To make a bevel cut, follow the same proce-dure with the board placed on edge *(inset)*.

MITER-BOX CLAMP

TRICKS OF THE TRADE

Cutting a Shallow Bevel

To cut a board at an angle greater than 45 degrees, mark the cutting line on the stock and place it in the miter box. Adjust the saw blade as close to the cutting line as possi-ble, then position the stock to align the cutting line with the blade just to the waste side; clamp the board in place with a wood pad for protec-tion. Wedge a piece of scrap wood in the gap between the back of the miter box and the stock, and clamp it in place to brace the board. Start the cut with several short strokes, holding the board firmly to keep it from moving while you are establishing the kerf.

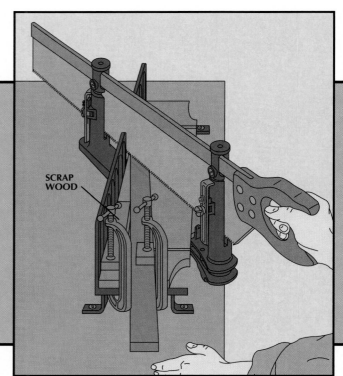

SCRAP WOOD

BEVEL AND COMPOUND CUTS WITH A CIRCULAR SAW

1. Setting the blade angle.
◆ Set a T-bevel to the angle of the cut *(page 28)*.
◆ With the saw unplugged, adjust the blade to its maximum cutting depth, then loosen the protractor nut on the saw's blade-angle scale.
◆ Holding the handle of the T-bevel firmly against the bottom of the base plate, retract the blade guard and tilt the base plate so the saw blade lies flat against the blade of the T-bevel *(right)*.
◆ Tighten the protractor nut to lock the setting.

A blade angle of 50 degrees is the maximum for most circular saws. To cut larger angles, use a miter box with a backsaw *(opposite)* or a handsaw alone.

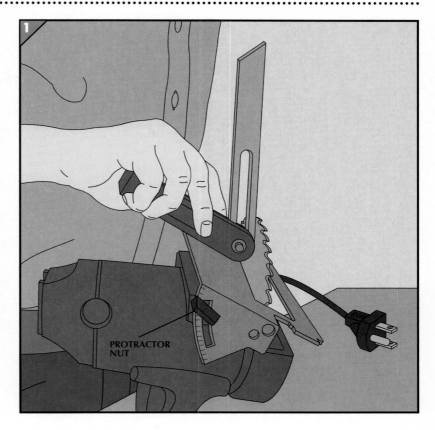

2. Making the cut.
◆ Mark a cutting line on the board—perpendicular to the edge for a bevel cut, or at the desired angle for a compound cut.
◆ Attach a straight-edge cutting guide to the board as you would for an angled cut *(page 29)*, then cut the board *(left)*.

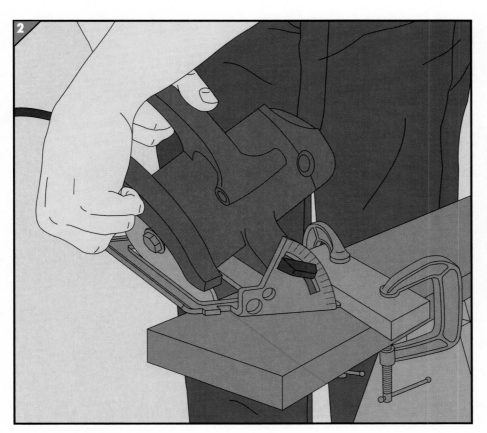

CUTTING WITH A RADIAL-ARM SAW

Setting the saw for miter cuts.

◆ For a typical miter cut, loosen the miter lock and swing the arm to the right to the desired angle *(right)*. Most radial-arm saws will lock automatically at 45 degrees; to set a different angle, release the lock and move it again.

◆ Position the board against the fence with your left hand so the blade will cut on the waste side of the cutting line.

◆ Make the cut as for a crosscut *(pages 19-20)*.

To cut a miter at the opposite angle, flip the board over and cut as described above. If the angle cannot be cut by turning the board over—as for a board with a molded edge—move the arm to the left *(inset)*. Since the motor does not come out as far with the arm in this position, when sawing wider boards you may need to move the fence to the back of the table *(page 35, Step 1)*.

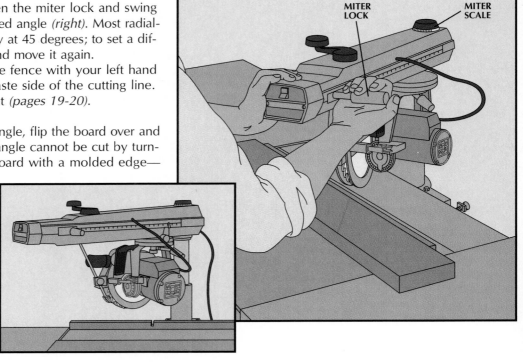

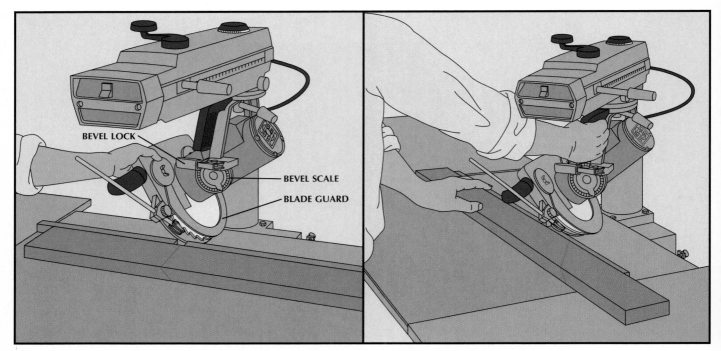

Making bevel and compound cuts.

◆ For a bevel cut, raise the arm of the saw, release the bevel lock, and tilt the blade to the correct angle *(above, left)*. Tighten the bevel lock.

◆ Check that the blade guard has enough play so it will not jam when it is pulled across the fence; if necessary, clean the guard of sawdust and lubricate it.

◆ Make the cut as you would a crosscut *(pages 19-20)*. If the guard jams, stop the saw immediately, and free it before continuing.

For a compound cut, swivel the arm as for a miter and tilt the blade for a bevel *(above, right)*, then make the cut.

Panels are difficult to cut mainly because of their size—they are sold almost exclusively in 4- by 8-foot sheets. Working with supports and guides can make the job much easier.

Straightedge Guides: A long board clamped across a panel can guide a circular saw to make an accurate crosscut. A two-piece jig, assembled from particleboard *(below)*, is ideal for repeat cuts. Two sturdy sawhorses are generally adequate support for crosscutting a panel *(page 34)*. For ripping, add 2-by-4s between the sawhorses to prevent the panel from sagging *(page 34)*.

To cut panels on a radial-arm saw, set up extension tables the same height as the saw table on both sides of it. A third extension table may be needed to support wide waste pieces. Although a radial-arm saw already has a guide—the fence—for ripping, add another guide for wide crosscuts *(pages 35-36)*.

Choosing a Blade: The materials and glues used in the manufacture of panels dull standard blades quickly. A carbide-tipped combination blade is better, but yields a relatively rough cut; your best choice is a carbide-tipped blade designed especially for plywood, particleboard, and other panels.

 TOOLS

Electric drill	Sawhorses
Counterbore bit	Radial-arm saw
Tape measure	Screwdriver	Extension
Circular saw	Utility knife	tables
C-clamps	Hammer	

 **MATERIALS**

2 x 4s
Wood screws ($\frac{3}{4}$", $1\frac{1}{4}$" No. 8)
Common nails (3")
Varnish
Particleboard ($\frac{3}{4}$")
Hardboard ($\frac{1}{4}$")
Lumber for guide (1" or 2" thick)

 SAFETY TIPS

Goggles prevent injury to your eyes when you are driving nails or operating a power tool.

A CROSSCUTTING GUIDE FOR A CIRCULAR SAW

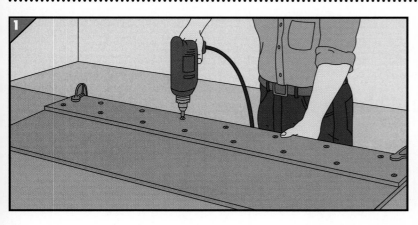

1. Assembling the jig.
◆ Cut a 4-inch by 4-foot strip from the factory-cut edge of a $\frac{3}{4}$-inch particleboard panel. Cut a second length, this one 12 inches wide.
◆ Align the two pieces so that the factory-cut edge of the narrow piece divides the width of the wider piece. Clamp the strips to a work surface.
◆ Countersink pilot holes for $1\frac{1}{4}$-inch No. 8 wood screws in a zigzag pattern along the edges of the narrow strips, then fasten the pieces together *(left)*.
◆ Varnish the jig to reduce warping.

2. Customizing the jig for a saw.
◆ Clamp the jig to the work surface so the wide strip overhangs the end of the table and the blade of a circular saw clears the table when its base plate is against the edge of the narrow strip.
◆ Riding the saw's base plate along the edge of the narrow strip, trim the wide piece along its entire length *(right)*.

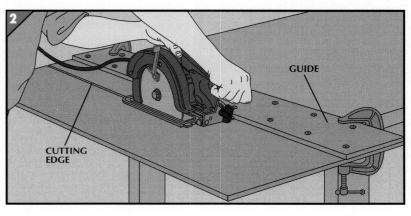

GUIDE

CUTTING EDGE

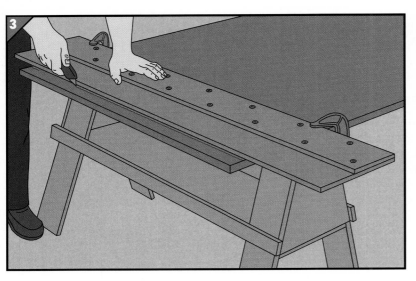

3. Crosscutting a panel with the jig.

◆ Make a cutting mark at both edges of the panel, align the trimmed edge of the jig with the marks so the saw blade will cut just to the waste side of the cutting line, and clamp the jig to the panel. Score the panel along the edge of the jig with a utility knife to reduce tearout *(left)*.

◆ Set the blade depth to account for the combined thickness of the jig and the panel.

◆ Cut the panel as in Step 2, running the saw along the edge of the jig's narrow strip. As you reach about 12 inches from the end of the cut, have a helper support the waste piece if it appears likely to break off before the cut is finished.

MAKING PRECISE RIP CUTS

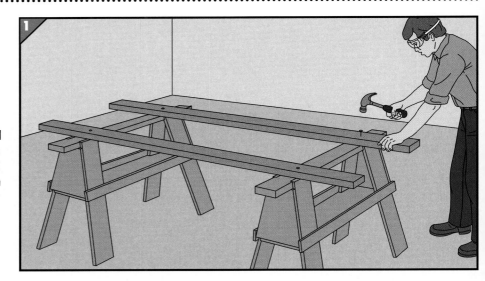

1. Building a panel support.

◆ Set two sawhorses at a distance apart about 2 feet less than the length of the panel to be cut.

◆ Fasten a 2-by-4 as long as the panel to the sawhorses with 3-inch common nails, then add another 2-by-4 parallel to the first and about 3 feet away from it *(right)*.

◆ Set the panel on the 2-by-4s.

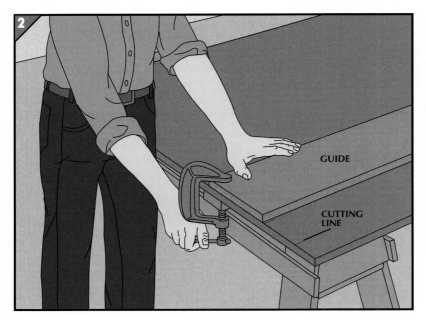

GUIDE

CUTTING
LINE

2. Ripping the panel.

◆ Mark a cutting line at both ends of the panel, then make a second set of marks, offsetting them from the first by the distance from the saw blade to the left-hand edge of its base plate.

◆ To make a guide for the saw, cut a 10-inch by 8-foot strip from the factory-cut edge of a sheet of $\frac{3}{4}$-inch particleboard.

◆ Place the guide on the panel, align it with the second set of marks so the saw will cut just to the waste side of the cutting line, and clamp it in place *(left)*.

◆ Cut the panel as you would for a crosscut *(Step 3, above)*.

CROSSCUTTING WITH A RADIAL-ARM SAW

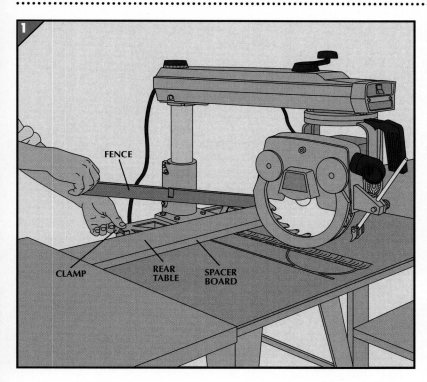

FENCE

CLAMP **REAR TABLE** **SPACER BOARD**

1. Extending the saw table.

◆ Move the fence closer to the back of the table by loosening the clamps behind the table, removing the fence, and sliding the rear table and spacer board—which is removable, allowing for the use of a wider fence—toward the front.

◆ Position the fence between the clamps and the rear table *(left)*, and tighten the clamps.

◆ Cut a piece of $\frac{1}{4}$-inch hardboard to cover the rear table and spacer board. Drill countersunk holes for $\frac{3}{4}$-inch No. 8 wood screws away from the path of the blade's travel, and fasten the hardboard in place.

◆ Set up an extension table on each side of the saw. To bring these tables to the same height as the saw table, trim or shim their legs as necessary.

If you will be attaching a guide to an extension table, as in Step 2 *(below)*, bolt the table to the floor or screw it to the saw table.

GUIDE

2. Setting up for a crosscut.

◆ Position the saw's yoke correctly for a crosscut *(page 20)*.

◆ Mark a cutting line across the panel, then slide it onto the saw table against the fence and align the blade just to the waste side of the line.

◆ Butt a straight guide against the edge of the panel and clamp it to both edges of the extension or saw table *(above)*. Pull the panel away from the blade.

◆ Pull the yoke toward the front of the arm and lock it in place. Lower the blade into the kerf in the table cover.

◆ Adjust the antikickback fingers so they rest $\frac{1}{8}$ inch below the top of the panel *(page 26, Step 3)*.

3. Cutting the panel.

◆ Place the front edge of the panel on the front of the saw table and against the guide, then start the motor. Feed the panel into the blade until it contacts the fence *(left)*.

◆ Turn off the saw and remove the panel. Turn it end for end and butt the same edge against the straightedge.

◆ Feed the panel into the blade the same way to complete the cut.

RIPPING TO WIDTH

Cutting the panel.

◆ Turn the yoke to the out-rip position *(page 25, Step 1)* and set the fence in the rear position *(page 35, Step 1)*.

◆ Place the panel to the left of the saw with its edge against the fence. Align the blade to the waste side of the cutting line on the panel and lock the motor in place. Adjust the blade guard and antikickback fingers *(pages 25-26, Steps 2-3)*.

◆ Start the motor and, with your left hand on the back of the panel and your right hand pressing it against the fence, feed the panel into the blade *(right)*.

If the blade starts to bind, turn off the saw and insert a kerf splitter into the cut *(page 23)*.

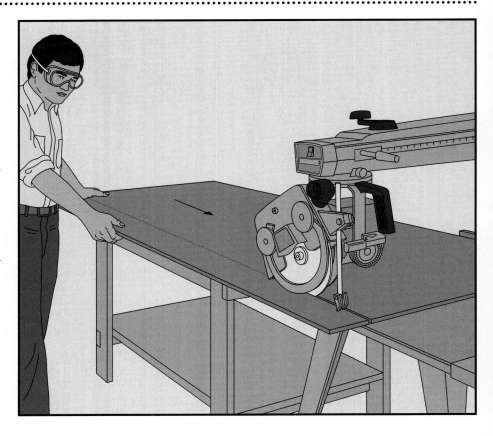

Cutting curves in wood is not as simple as making straight cuts, but with special tools and techniques, you can saw irregular outlines with great precision.

Handsaws: In cramped quarters or in situations where a power saw cannot be used, use a handsaw designed specifically for cutting curves such as the compass saw. The keyhole saw *(below)* is a smaller variation, designed for finer work. Both saws come with an assortment of blades designed for different materials. The blades are tapered, with narrow tips suited for tight turns and cutouts. The coping saw has a delicate blade and a limited cutting range; it is best for finish joints in woodwork and fine, intricate scrollwork.

Power Tools: A saber saw with variable-speed control is the most convenient power saw for cutting curves *(page 38)*. A $\frac{1}{4}$-inch-wide blade with 8 to 10 points per inch is suitable for most jobs; for very fine work, select a blade with 12 or 14 points per inch. Specialized blades are also available. For smoother cuts or for sawing odd-shaped items that cannot be clamped, a band saw is a good alternative *(page 41)*.

Cutting a Curve Accurately: Follow the marked line carefully and never force the blade—under excess pressure, a handsaw blade will buckle and a saber saw blade may snap. Saber saws cut on the upstroke and thus tend to splinter the upper surface of the wood; if possible, cut with the poorer-quality side of the board facing up. Or, cover the cutting lines with transparent tape to minimize the damage.

TOOLS

Sawhorses
Electric drill
Compass saw
Saber saw
C-clamps

SAFETY TIPS

Protect your eyes with goggles when operating a power tool.

SAWING AN INTERIOR OUTLINE BY HAND

Using a compass or keyhole saw.
◆ Set the board on sawhorses.
◆ Drill a $\frac{3}{4}$-inch starter hole through the waste area.
◆ Insert the tip of the saw blade into the hole and make a few short, vertical strokes to start the cut.
◆ When you reach the cutting line, make short strokes with the narrow tip of the blade to cut around sharp turns. Then lower the blade to a 45-degree angle and follow the cutting line with long, even strokes, applying light pressure *(right)*.

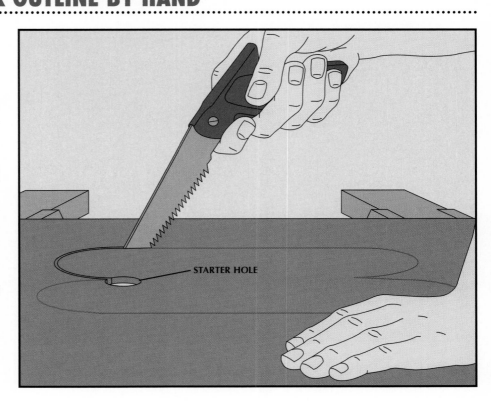

STARTER HOLE

Cutting broad and sharp curves.
◆ With wood pads to protect the surface, clamp the board to a worktable with the cutting line overhanging the edge.
◆ Keeping the saber saw's base plate flat against the wood, guide the saw forward along the broad curves of the cutting line; bypass any sharp turns to avoid forcing the saw or pushing the blade sideways *(right)*.
◆ Once the large waste piece falls away, remove the remaining waste from the V-shaped sections with separate cuts from each side into the point.

To ease the saw around a curve, you can make radial cuts across the waste area, then saw along the cutting line; the waste will drop off in pieces as you saw, giving the blade more room to turn *(inset)*.

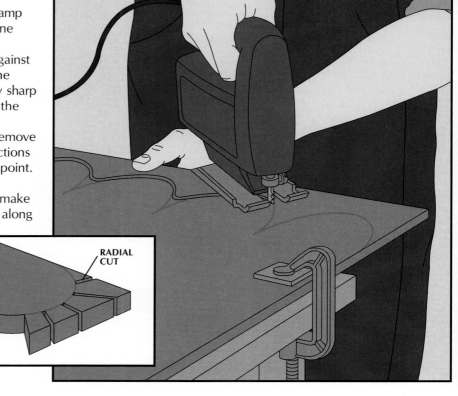

RADIAL CUT

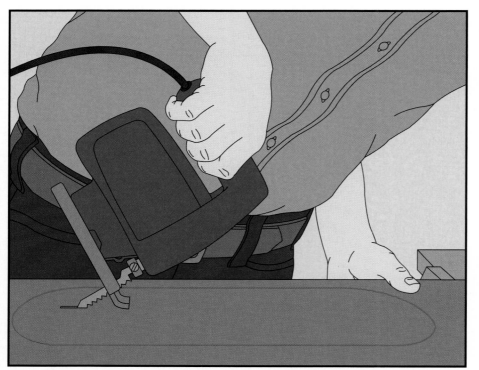

Making a plunge cut.
◆ Clamp the workpiece to sawhorses.
◆ With the saw motor off and the blade clear of the wood, rest the front edge of the base plate on the waste area near the marked cutting line.
◆ Turn on the saw and, pressing firmly on the front of the base plate, slowly lower the back of the saw until the blade contacts and cuts through the wood *(left)*.
◆ When the base plate rests flat on the wood, saw to the line and make the cut as described above.

Three Stationary Saws

In addition to the radial-arm saw, three other types of stationary power tools—the table saw, power miter saw, and band saw—are common in home workshops. Each tool excels at several types of cuts.

With each of these saws, take the general safety precautions that apply to all power tools.

The Table Saw: Consisting of a stationary circular blade that projects through a slot in its metal worktable, the table saw is more convenient than the radial-arm saw for ripping boards, mainly because of its adjustable rip fence *(below)*. With its miter gauge, you can make accurate miter and compound angle cuts *(page 40)*. However, because the wood must be moved past the blade, large panels are difficult to handle on the table saw; such operations are best done with table extensions and a helper.

The Power Miter Saw: Also known as a motorized miter box or chop saw, this tool crosscuts more accurately and with less setup than any other tool, and is prized for its ability to cut precise 45-degree miters. Most models, however, can crosscut boards only up to 12 inches wide; for miter cuts, boards must be even narrower. Some saws cut miters when the board is laid flat and bevels when it is held on edge *(page 40)*. Special compound-miter saws cut compound angles as well as standard miters.

The Band Saw: Producing smoother and more precise curved cuts than a saber saw, the band saw *(page 41)* turns a thin, flexible blade around two wheels and through a worktable. The saw's great depth of cut—up to 6 inches on most models—allows you to crosscut thick lumber, or to resaw—slice a thick board on edge into thinner strips. Check and adjust the blade clearance from time to time *(page 41)*, or whenever a new blade is installed.

TOOLS

Table saw
Push stick
Screwdriver
Power miter saw
Band saw
Hex wrench

MATERIALS

Stock for miter
   gauge extension
Wood screws (No. 8)

SAFETY TIPS

Wear goggles when operating a power saw.

SIMPLE CUTS WITH A TABLE SAW

Ripping a board.

◆ Set up an extension table to support the pieces as they are cut.

◆ Place the board on the saw table and align the blade to the waste side of the cutting line.

◆ Butt the rip fence against the board and lock the fence in place.

◆ Standing to one side of the blade, position your left hand on the table about halfway between the blade guard and the table edge to keep the board pressed lightly against the fence. Hook the fingers of your right hand over the fence.

◆ Advance the board with your right hand while keeping your left hand in place *(right)*. If either hand comes within 6 inches of the blade, use a push stick to move the workpiece past the blade. If the blade binds, stop the saw and insert a kerf splitter in the cut *(page 23)*.

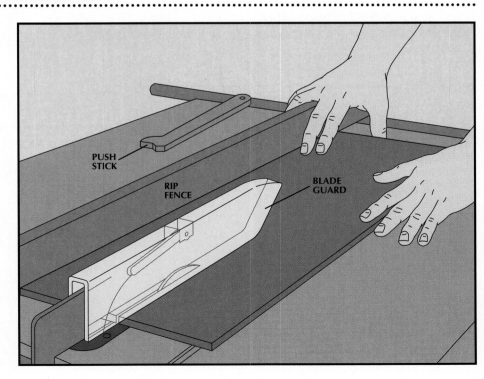

PUSH STICK

RIP FENCE

BLADE GUARD

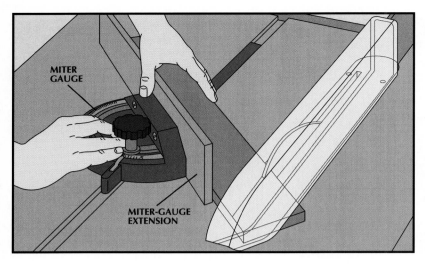

Cutting a miter.

◆ With No. 8 wood screws, fasten a board to the miter gauge as an extension to provide more bearing surface for the workpiece.
◆ Set the miter gauge to the desired angle.
◆ Holding the board against the extension with your left hand so the blade is aligned with the cutting line on the waste side, push the miter gauge forward with your right hand *(left)*. Hold the board tightly against the extension to prevent the blade from pulling the board off course during the cut.

For a compound cut, tilt the blade to the desired bevel angle and make the cut in the same way.

USING A POWER MITER SAW

A handy hybrid.

A power miter saw is a cross between a circular saw and a miter box. The saw pivots up and down on a fixed axis to cut boards placed against its fence. The movable base allows you to set the angle of the blade relative to the fence, as indicated on the scale.

The saw can swivel about 48 degrees right or left. On most models, the blade automatically locks when it stops at the 0-, $22\frac{1}{2}$-, and 45-degree positions. As the blade is lowered into the wood, the clear plastic blade guard rises and the sawdust is carried away from the work surface through a dust spout. The assembly can be bolted to a workbench through the predrilled holes in the base.

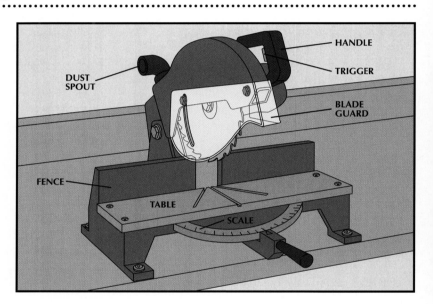

Making an angled cut.

◆ Move the control arm to set the blade to the desired angle. Unless the base automatically locks in place, secure it—usually with a latch or screw on the control arm.
◆ Place the board on the table against the fence, and align the waste side of the cutting line with the blade. Keep the ends of long pieces level with wood blocks.
◆ Holding the board firmly against the fence with your hand at least 8 inches from the blade, grip the handle with your other hand, depress the trigger, and slowly pull the blade down into the wood *(left)*.
◆ When the cut is completed, raise the blade and release the trigger, but keep your hands in place until the blade comes to a complete stop.

⚠ **CAUTION** *Do not attempt to cut pieces shorter than 8 inches—the wood might be wrenched from your hands.*

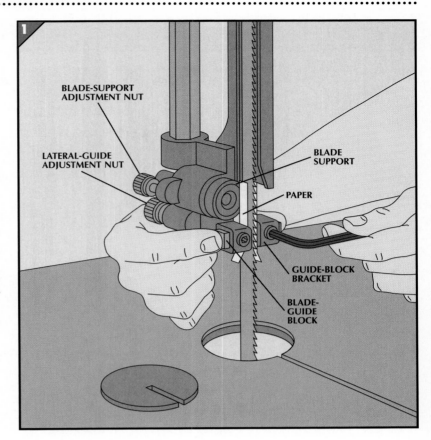

1. Adjusting the blade clearance.

◆ Turn the blade-support adjustment nut until the blade support just touches the blade, then back off the support slightly to set a small gap between the support and the back of the blade.

◆ Turn the lateral-guide adjustment nut to position the front edges of the guide blocks just behind the gullets between the teeth of the blade.

◆ To set the clearance between the guide blocks and the blade, loosen the brackets with a hex wrench. Wrap a piece of paper around the blade and press the blocks together against the paper until they hold it in place without pinching the blade. Tighten the brackets *(right)* and remove the paper.

Labels in figure 1:
BLADE-SUPPORT ADJUSTMENT NUT
LATERAL-GUIDE ADJUSTMENT NUT
BLADE SUPPORT
PAPER
GUIDE-BLOCK BRACKET
BLADE-GUIDE BLOCK

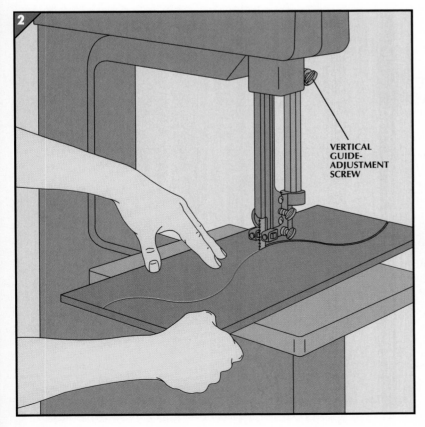

Labels in figure 2:
VERTICAL GUIDE-ADJUSTMENT SCREW

2. Making the cut.

◆ With the vertical-guide adjustment screw, set the blade guides $\frac{1}{4}$ inch above the board.

◆ Set the board on the table, align the blade just to the waste side of the cutting line, and guide the board through the blade along the cutting line with both hands—your right hand near the back end pushing and steering and your left hand on the surface of the board to help with the finer movements and guidance *(left)*. Don't force the workpiece; let the saw dictate the pace—but don't go too slowly or the blade will burn the wood. At all times, position your hands so that your fingers would not be in line with the blade if the board were to suddenly move forward.

◆ If the blade starts to bind at a very sharp turn, run the blade off of the edge of the board through the waste area, then come back in to cut from another angle.

◆ At the end of the cut, turn off the saw and leave the board on the table until the blade has stopped.

A Multitude of Holes

There are a variety of ways to create holes, from boring a pilot hole with a small twist bit to plunge-cutting with a circular saw for a rectangular opening. Like any other facet of working with wood, drilling and cutting holes require mastering certain techniques to do the task properly; this chapter illustrates a variety of these methods.

The skill and precision required for cutting wood is also needed for drilling holes, but you can avoid many problems if you use the right tools and techniques. If you do make a hole at the wrong place or the wrong angle, you can often correct it by gluing in a tightly fitting dowel, then redrilling the hole.

Hand Drills: For small jobs, particularly in hard-to-reach places, you may want to use a hand drill. Choose an egg-beater type to drill small holes and a brace for larger ones *(page 47)*.

Electric Drills: The most practical model for home carpentry is a $\frac{3}{8}$-inch variable-speed reversible portable drill *(page 46)*. Select one with a double-insulated case—to prevent electric shock—and a lockable reverse switch.

The stationary drill press *(pages 50-51)* is faster, more precise, and more versatile than other drills, and is perfect for repetitive tasks such as boring a set of holes for dowels or shelf supports; however, it cannot handle large panels.

Guides and Jigs: The biggest challenge when drilling is controlling the bit after it enters the wood. To regulate the depth of the hole, you can wrap tape around the bit at the correct depth, or use a factory-made stop collar or a wood block *(page 101)*. A variety of shop-made and commercial jigs can help you drill holes straight or at an angle *(pages 48-49)*.

 TOOLS

Electric drill	Awl	T-bevel
Bits	Clamps	Handsaw
Combination	Egg-beater drill	Drill press
square	Ratchet brace	Wrench
	Drill guide	
	Dowel jig	

 **MATERIALS**

Support board Wood block

 **SAFETY TIPS**

Protect your eyes with goggles when operating a power tool.

CHOOSING THE RIGHT BIT

TWIST BIT   BRAD-POINT BIT

Bits for small holes.

Two simple bits are generally used to drill holes up to $\frac{1}{2}$ inch wide. The all-purpose twist bit bores through plastic and metal as well as wood. The brad-point bit is preferred for dowel holes and exposed woodwork. The point at the center of the shaft guides the bit, while sharp spurs score the perimeter of the hole to eliminate splintering.

Bits for holes up to 1 inch wide.

When drilling larger holes, three bits are particularly effective. The spade bit, the most versatile and inexpensive of the three, is used with an electric drill; however, it tends to wander in deep holes and often leaves ragged edges.

The single-twist auger bit can be used in a hand brace or a large electric drill. Slower than a spade bit, it is easier to control and leaves a cleaner, more precise hole. As the bit is pulled into the wood by the feed screw at the tip, spurs on the outside score the hole's edges and the cutters scrape away wood chips.

An electrician's bit works on the same principle as the auger bit but is used for deeper holes and rougher work. It is more flexible because it has no solid central shaft.

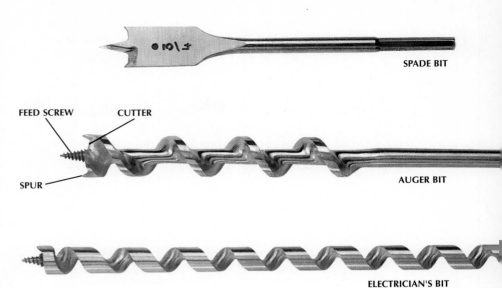

SPADE BIT

FEED SCREW   CUTTER

SPUR

AUGER BIT

ELECTRICIAN'S BIT

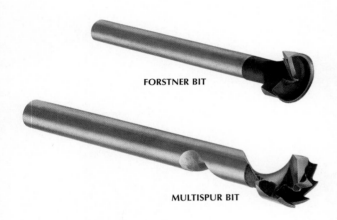

FORSTNER BIT

MULTISPUR BIT

Special-purpose bits.

For cutting large holes with very clean edges, two specially designed bits are ideal. The Forstner bit has a flat, disc-shaped head and sharp outer rim. The outer edges dig into the wood, allowing it to drill at an angle to a board's surface without sliding off, and to hold a position even when there is a void under the point of the bit. This tool makes flat-bottomed holes—an advantage when you need a large counterbore or are drilling partway through a board.

A multispur or sawtooth bit has a sharp tip encircled by a ring of teeth. This bit cuts as cleanly as a Forstner, but the sawlike edge makes it well suited to cutting wider holes up to about 3 inches, or drilling through plywood or paneling.

Countersink bits.

When a job calls for screwheads to be flush with or lower than the surface, choose a countersink bit. The combination countersink-counterbore bit *(near right)*, intended for use with an electric drill, in one step drills a pilot hole, bevels the top of the hole for a screwhead and, if required, counterbores a hole for a wooden plug. This tool is essentially a stop collar slipped over the shank of a bit and fastened with a setscrew *(page 101)*; the depth of the pilot hole is determined by the position of the collar on the shank.

If a pilot hole has already been drilled, if the screwhead is too large for a combination bit, or if you need to countersink only a few holes, use a regular countersink designed for a hand brace *(center right)* or an electric drill *(far right)*.

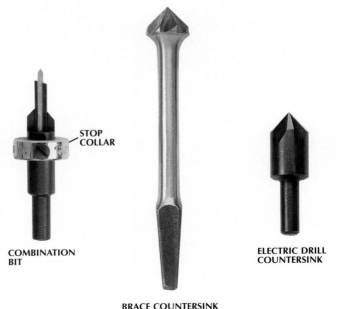

STOP COLLAR

COMBINATION BIT

BRACE COUNTERSINK

ELECTRIC DRILL COUNTERSINK

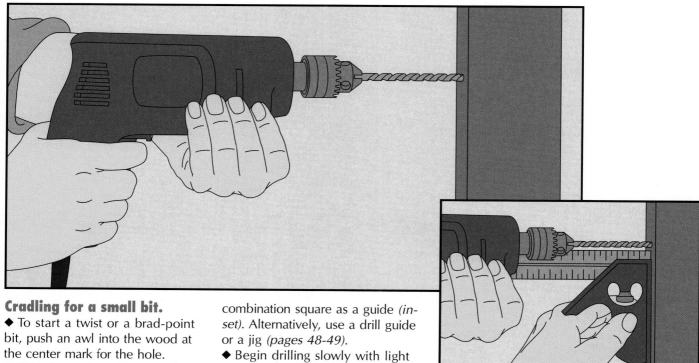

Cradling for a small bit.

◆ To start a twist or a brad-point bit, push an awl into the wood at the center mark for the hole.
◆ Grip the tool as shown and set the point of the bit in the awl hole *(above)*. To ensure that the bit is perfectly perpendicular, line it up by eye or have a helper hold a combination square as a guide *(inset)*. Alternatively, use a drill guide or a jig *(pages 48-49)*.
◆ Begin drilling slowly with light pressure until the bit starts to turn, then increase the speed of the drill to its maximum and bear down firmly.
◆ When the bit has drilled almost to the full depth of the board, reduce the pressure but maintain the same speed until the hole is completed.

Steadying a large bit.

◆ Indent the center of the hole with an awl.
◆ For a bit with large cutting edges, such as a spade bit, grasp the top of the drill securely, press the bit firmly into the awl hole and begin to bore at a fairly high speed *(above)*. If the bit binds momentarily, maintain speed but pull the drill back slightly, then press again.
◆ When the bit nears the other side of the board, reduce pressure and brace yourself; the drill may jerk and bind as it breaks through.

With an auger bit, start boring as you would with a spade bit, but at a slightly slower speed. If the motor labors, press the trigger to maintain speed. When you near the end of the hole, reduce the speed; when the feed screw breaks through, bear down with additional force to complete the hole.

WORKING BY HAND

Using an egg-beater drill.
◆ Clamp the board to a worktable.
◆ Push the tip of an awl into the workpiece at the center mark for the hole.
◆ Set the bit point in the awl hole, press the tool lightly against the wood, and turn the crank clockwise *(right)*.
◆ When the bit breaks through the board, continue to crank clockwise as you pull the bit out. (Cranking counterclockwise will release the bit from the chuck.)

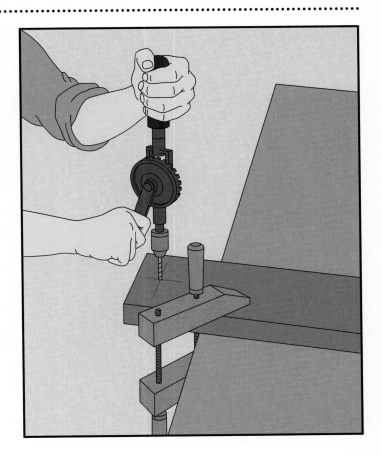

A ratchet brace.
Where there is too little space to align an electric drill properly, work with a ratchet brace, adjusting the setting for a clockwise sweep.
◆ Push an awl into the wood at the center mark for the hole.
◆ Set the feed screw of the auger bit into the awl hole and holding the brace very steady, press hard on its head with one hand, and slowly swing the handle in half circles until the bit begins to bore *(above)*.
◆ When the bit breaks through the board, reverse the ratchet adjustment and swing the handle to back the bit out.

BRACES FOR TIGHT SPOTS

Some braces are designed to be used in areas that would be too cramped for a conventional brace like the one at left. The close-quarter or joist brace *(near right)* has a handle set at a 90-degree angle to the bit, enabling the tool to be cranked while the head is held directly over the hole. The short-throw brace *(far right)* is essentially a standard brace with a smaller swing radius—a helpful feature in restricted spaces where the 12-inch swing of the typical standard brace handle would be too wide.

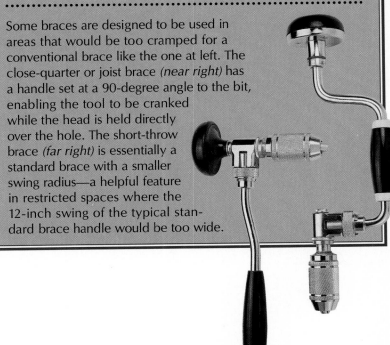

GUIDES AND JIGS FOR PRECISION WORK

A hand-held drill guide.
This device ensures perfect right-angle drilling. Its revolving selector can accommodate common bit sizes.
◆ Turn the selector so the hole matching the diameter of bit to be used is in the uppermost position.
◆ Make an alignment line on the wood to center the hole; to locate its vertical position, make an awl mark along the line. To pinpoint the hole in the desired spot, line up the point on the guide with the alignment line and the hole in the jig with the awl mark. Insert the drill bit into the hole in the guide and bore the hole *(right).*

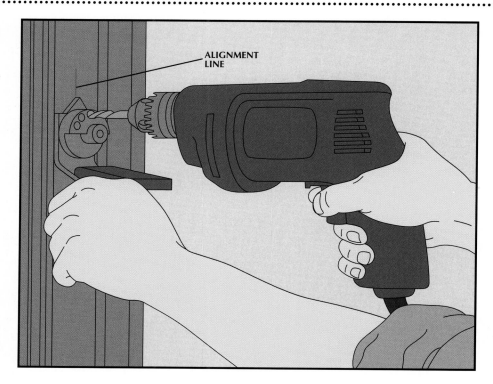

ALIGNMENT LINE

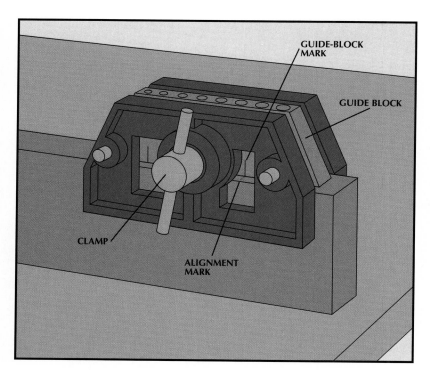

GUIDE-BLOCK MARK

GUIDE BLOCK

CLAMP

ALIGNMENT MARK

A self-centering dowel jig.
The guide block of the jig shown at left has holes for several common dowel sizes and is automatically centered over the board's edge by a clamp.
◆ With a combination square, mark a line across the board's edge at the desired location of the hole.
◆ Set the jig on the board's edge, aligning the guide-block mark corresponding to the correct dowel size with the mark on the board's edge, and tighten the clamp.
◆ Drill the hole with a twist bit or a brad-point bit.

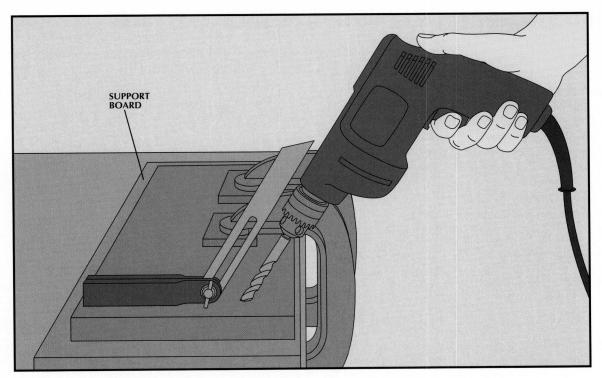

SUPPORT
BOARD

Guiding an angled hole with a T-bevel.
◆ Place the workpiece on top of a support board and clamp both to a work surface.
◆ With an awl, indent the center of the hole to be drilled.

◆ Adjust a T-bevel to the desired angle, then line up its handle beside the marked hole.
◆ Set the bit in the awl hole and drill, keeping the bit parallel to the blade of the T-bevel while you work *(above)*.

A guide block for an angled hole.
A simple jig made from a small block of wood will enable you to drill angled holes quickly and accurately.
◆ To make the jig, use the same bit you will use for the angled hole to bore a hole straight through a block of wood.
◆ Cut one end of the block at the same angle as the hole you will be drilling.
◆ Saw a notch in one side of the block to facilitate clamping.
◆ Place a support board underneath the workpiece and, with an awl, mark the center of the hole to be bored on the workpiece.
◆ Before putting the bit in the drill, insert it in the jig and set the bit point in the awl hole. Clamp the jig in place, then extract the bit from the jig.
◆ Secure the bit in the drill and bore the hole *(right)*.

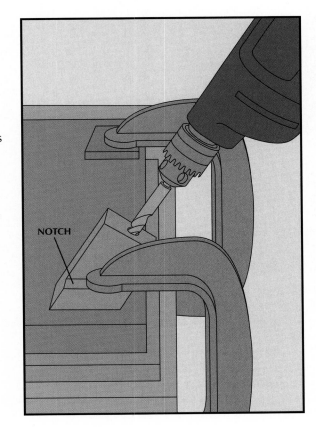

NOTCH

BORING STRAIGHT HOLES WITH A STATIONARY TOOL

1. Adjusting the drill-press table.

◆ With the bit in the drill chuck, clamp the workpiece and a support board to the drill-press table.
◆ Holding the table, loosen the locking handle that fastens it to the column, then move the table by simultaneously raising or lowering it and swinging it from side to side. When the tip of the drill bit is about $\frac{1}{4}$ inch above the board, tighten the locking handle and move the safety collar on the column to just beneath the table.
◆ Adjust the stop nut and the lock nut on the calibrated stop rod to set the depth of the planned hole *(right)*.

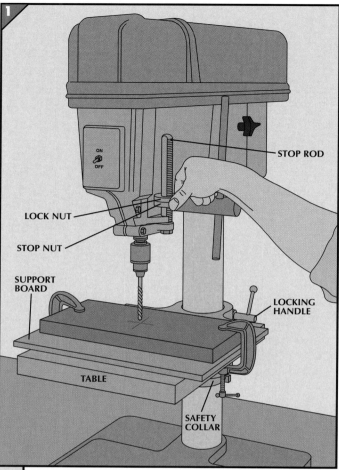

STOP ROD

LOCK NUT

STOP NUT

SUPPORT BOARD

LOCKING HANDLE

TABLE

SAFETY COLLAR

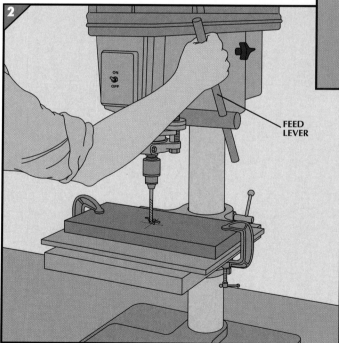

FEED LEVER

2. Drilling the hole.

◆ With the drill turned off, loosen the clamps holding the workpiece and turn the feed lever until the bit almost touches the wood.
◆ Shift the workpiece to place the center of the planned hole directly beneath the tip of the bit, then clamp it.
◆ With the bit above the workpiece, turn the motor on and slowly lower the bit into the wood, using light pressure on the feed lever *(above)*.

A STAND FOR A PORTABLE DRILL

When fitted into a drill stand, a portable electric drill can perform many of the functions of a press at a fraction of the price. The model shown at right features a tiltable work table that will hold flat as well as cylindrical-shaped workpieces.

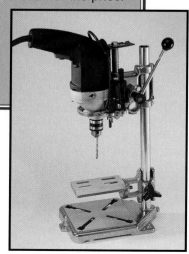

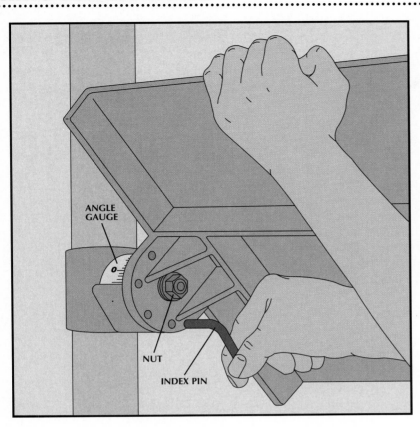

ANGLE GAUGE

NUT

INDEX PIN

Tilting the drill-press table.

◆ If your drill-press table pivots on the clamp that fastens it to the column, as in the model shown at left, loosen the nut at the base of the table; remove the index pin from its hole in the base, and tilt the table to the desired angle.

◆ To drill a hole at an angle of 45, 90, 135, or 180 degrees, slide the index pin through the hole for the angle and tighten the nut (left). For other angles, set the index pin aside, align the arrow on the table top with the correct reading on the angle gauge, and tighten the nut.

TRICKS OF THE TRADE

A Homemade Tilting Table Jig

If your drill press does not have a tilting table, you can make a jig that will allow you to bore angled holes. Cut two pieces of $\frac{3}{4}$-inch plywood to $9\frac{1}{2}$ by 11 inches and hinge them together lengthwise. Fasten $8\frac{1}{2}$-inch metal desk-lid slides to the opposite sides of the boards with hanger bolts and wing nuts.

To use the table, secure the base to the drill-press table with C-clamps, raise the upper board to the angle you want, checking with a T-bevel, then lock the upper board by tightening the wing nuts on the slides. Position the workpiece under the bit and fasten it to the angled table with C-clamps, then drill the hole.

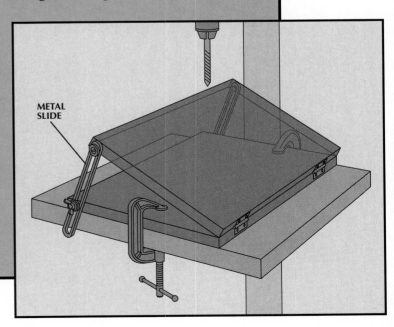

METAL SLIDE

Although spade and auger bits can bore holes that are as wide as $1\frac{1}{2}$ inches, most holes greater than 1 inch in diameter need a different set of tools.

Drilling: For holes between 1 and 3 inches in diameter, like those for door locksets or plumbing drains and vents, equip your electric drill with a hole saw. This hollow metal cylinder with sawlike teeth fits onto a separate shaft called a mandrel *(below)*, and can be paired with such accessories as bit extensions—some as long as 4 feet—for very deep or inaccessible holes.

To drill an odd-size hole or if you lack the right size hole saw, you can substitute a brace and an expansion bit *(opposite)*, which has a cutter that adjusts to a range of diameters.

Sawing: If you need to make a round hole larger than 3 inches, the compass saw *(page 37)* will serve, but a faster tool is a saber saw, used freehand or with a guide that guarantees perfect circles *(opposite)*.

Rectangular holes with sides up to 8 inches long can be cut with a saber saw as described on page 54, or by using the plunging technique on page 38; those with sides greater than 8 inches are made more quickly with a portable circular saw *(page 54)*.

 TOOLS

Electric drill
Hole saw
Awl
Brace
Expansion bit
Saber saw and
   edge guide
Screwdriver
Circular saw
Compass saw

 SAFETY TIPS

Protect your eyes with goggles when operating power tools.

SPECIAL DRILL ATTACHMENTS

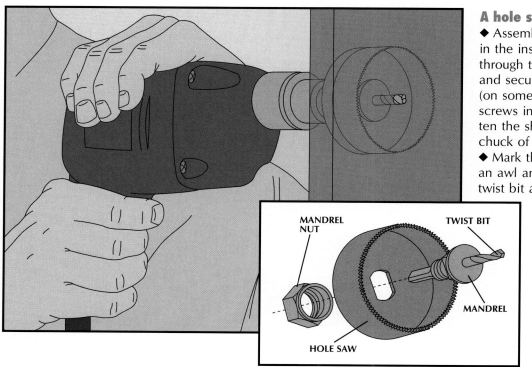

MANDREL NUT

TWIST BIT

MANDREL

HOLE SAW

A hole saw for an electric drill.
◆ Assemble the hole saw as shown in the inset. Slide the mandrel through the center of the hole saw and secure it with the mandrel nut (on some large saws, the mandrel screws into the hole saw), then fasten the shank of the mandrel in the chuck of the drill.
◆ Mark the center of the hole with an awl and start the hole with the twist bit at the end of the mandrel; when the saw begins to cut, grasp the top of the drill firmly *(left)*.
◆ To prevent the wood from splintering, when the twist bit breaks through the opposite surface, withdraw the saw and finish the job from the other side.

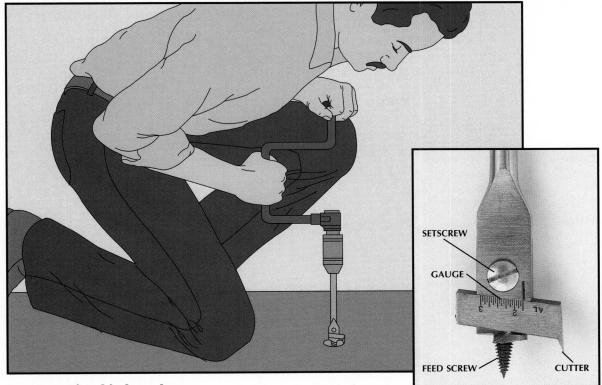

An expansion bit for a brace.

◆ An expansion bit *(inset)* can be adjusted to make holes of varying sizes. To set the size of the hole, loosen the setscrew at the head of the bit and slide the cutter to the diameter of the desired hole, as indicated on the cutter gauge, then tighten the setscrew; if precision is essential, check the cutter setting by drilling a trial hole.

◆ Install the bit in the brace and drill, taking care to keep the brace perfectly vertical so the cutter will shave away the wood evenly. As the hole deepens, bear down on the brace to ensure that the feed screw continues to pull *(above)*.

SAWS FOR ANY SIZE OPENING

A perfect circle with a saber saw.

◆ Drill a starter hole slightly larger than the saber-saw blade at the cutting line. Insert the blade in the hole.

◆ Slide the arm of a commercial edge guide through the slots in the saw's shoe, then drive a screw or nail through one of the holes in the end of the edge guide into the exact center of the planned hole.

◆ Lock the guide arm in place by tightening the setscrew *(right)*.

◆ Start the saw and cut the hole by pivoting the guide around the screw.

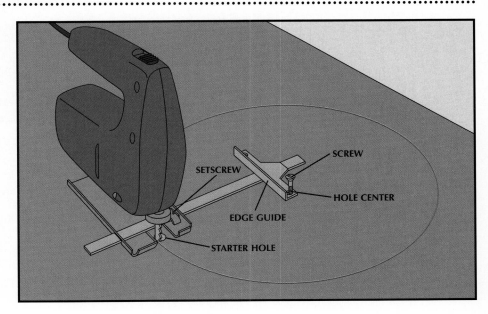

Cutting a rectangle with a saber saw.

◆ Drill a hole slightly larger than the saw blade at each corner.
◆ Insert the blade in one hole *(right)* and cut along the outline. When you reach the corner, turn the saw off.
◆ Make the cut along all the other sides in the same way.

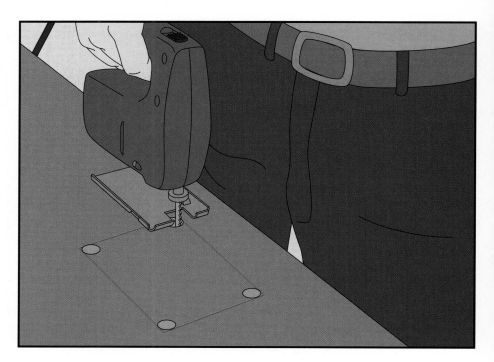

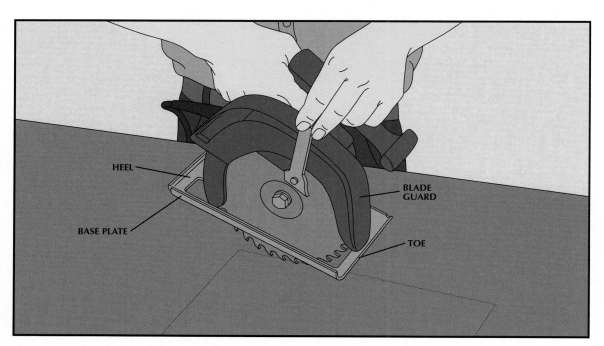

HEEL

BLADE
GUARD

BASE PLATE

TOE

A rectangular hole with a circular saw.

◆ Set the blade of the saw $\frac{1}{4}$ inch deeper than the thickness of the wood.
◆ Rest the toe of the saw on the workpiece, holding the heel and blade above the wood. Retract the blade guard and align the blade at the waste side of the cutting line on one side of the hole *(above).*
◆ Start the saw and, holding it very firmly, carefully lower the blade into the wood until the base plate rests flat on the surface; then guide the saw along the cutting line, stopping a few inches short of the corner.
◆ Remove the saw and cut the other sides of the hole the same way.
◆ Finish off the cuts with a compass saw.

⚠ **CAUTION** *Using this method requires special care. Grip the saw firmly and be prepared to turn it off if it goes out of control.*

Cutting Mortises

The holes known as mortises come in various forms. Some are quite shallow, such as those for door hinges. Others are deeper, like those in furniture, door, and window joints. Cutting these holes requires specialized tools.

Shallow Cuts: The traditional way of cutting shallow mortises is with a wood chisel *(below and pages 56-57)*.

The best chisels have a beveled edge and either a wood handle with a metal cap or a solid plastic handle. But for quicker results, many woodworkers rely on a router *(page 58)*.

Deep Mortises: An electric drill will quickly clean out most of the waste of a deep hole, leaving some paring to be performed by hand *(page 59)*. More precise is a drill press with a mortising attachment *(page 61)*. This device takes time to set up, but is well worth the effort if you have to cut numerous mortises. Although a standard router can be used for deep mortises, you will need to angle the tool on the surface and tilt it down to make a cut. With the more specialized plunge router *(page 60)*, simply rest the tool on the surface and push down to lower the bit.

 TOOLS

Utility knife
Butt gauge
Hammer
Wood chisels
Mallet
Router

Straight bit
Mortise gauge
Combination
    square
Electric drill
C-clamps
Handscrew
    clamps

Stop collar
Plunger router
Edge guide
Mortising bit
Drill press
Mortising
    attachment

 **MATERIALS**

Hardware
Lumber for support
    board, edge-guide
    extension

 SAFETY TIPS

Wear goggles when you are striking a chisel with a mallet and when operating a power tool. Add a dust mask for routing.

CHISELING A RECESS

1. Marking the mortise.

Position the hardware—in this example, the faceplate of a door catch—on the wood. To prevent splintering the surface when chiseling, score along the edges of the hardware with a utility knife, making repeated light strokes to cut the wood fiber *(left)*. If you plan to leave the corners curved for round-cornered hardware, use especially light strokes at the corners; if the knife point is pressed too hard, it will tend to follow a straight path between fibers and stray from the rounded outlines.

If you need to mark the location of a hinge, a butt gauge the same size as the hinge *(photograph)* will make quick work of the task. Positioned against the edge of the door, the gauge is then tapped with a hammer, driving its three sharp edges into the wood to outline the hinge.

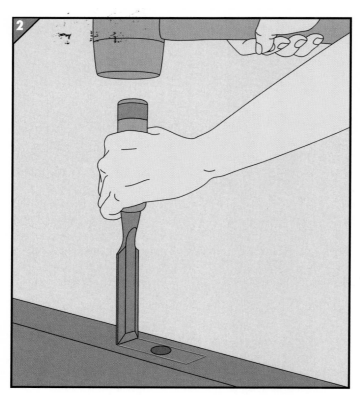

2. Cutting the edges.

◆ Select a bevel-edged chisel with a blade width equal to the mortise width. Set its cutting edge on one of the scored lines, with the bevel facing into the outlined area.

◆ Holding the blade perpendicular to the piece, tap the handle with a mallet *(left)*. Cut slightly deeper than the thickness of the hardware—you can gauge the depth of the cut directly on the chisel blade by holding your thumbnail at the junction of the blade and the wood, then pulling the chisel out of the cut.

◆ Repeat the cuts along the other scored lines.

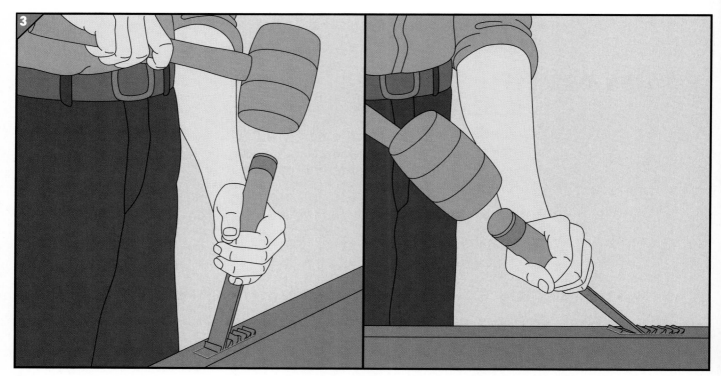

3. Scoring the mortise.

◆ Set the chisel's blade vertically across the outlined area, about $\frac{1}{4}$ inch from one end, with the bevel facing outward, then slant the chisel slightly toward the bevel side and away from the hand holding the mallet. Tap the chisel to a depth slightly less than the thickness of the hardware.

◆ Repeat this cut at $\frac{1}{4}$-inch intervals to within $\frac{1}{4}$ inch of the far end of the mortise *(above, left)*.

◆ Reverse the chisel and cut through the $\frac{1}{4}$-inch chips, holding the chisel so that the bevel is almost horizontal and is at the full depth of the mortise *(above, right)*.

◆ Reverse the chisel a second time to clear out the far end of the mortise.

GLEN ROCK
PUBLIC LIBRARY

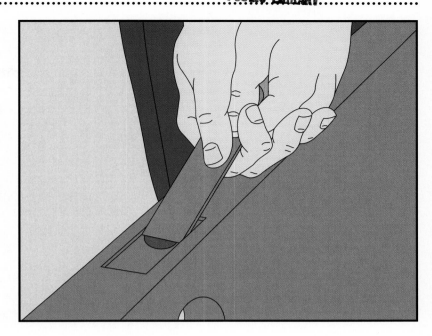

Paring a closed mortise.

◆ Hold the chisel, bevel down, with the heel of one hand against the end of the handle and the thumb of your other hand on the flat side of the blade. Make light shaving strokes parallel to the grain along the bottom of the mortise to produce a smooth, even surface *(right)*.

◆ Stop and test-fit the hardware occasionally to check the depth of the mortise.

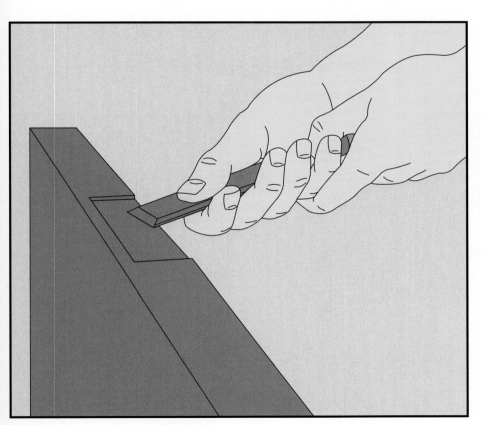

Paring an open mortise.

◆ Position the chisel, bevel up, at the open side of the mortise, setting the flat side of the blade even with the bottom of the mortise. Grip the chisel as you would for a closed mortise *(above)*, holding the index finger of your forward hand as far back from the cutting edge as the width of the mortise, so that with each stroke, you can stop the blade when the edge reaches the far side.

◆ Make light shaving strokes, working at about an 80-degree angle to the wood grain *(left)*.

ROUTING A SHALLOW MORTISE

1. Setting up for routing.

◆ Fit a straight bit in a router.
◆ Hold the tool with its base up, then adjust the depth of the bit to the thickness of the hardware you are using *(right)*.
◆ Score the outline with a utility knife *(page 55, Step 1)*.
◆ Cut the edges of the mortise *(page 56, Step 2)*.

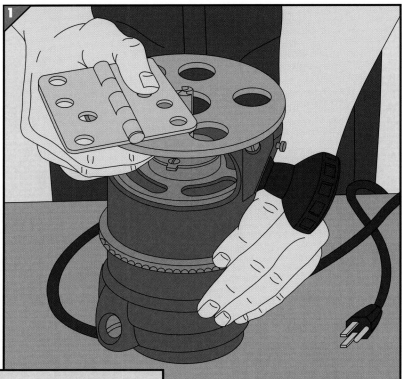

2. Routing out the wood.

◆ To make a closed mortise, set the router bit over the board at the center of the outline. Tilt the router slightly to raise the bit above the surface, then turn on the motor and slowly lower the bit into the wood *(above)*.

◆ With the base plate flat on the wood, guide the bit to remove the wood within the outlined area.

For an open mortise, start the cut at the edge of the board, as you would to rout a rabbet or dado *(page 81)*.

Router Safety

✔ Be sure to unplug the router when changing the bit.
✔ Keep the router bits clean and sharp; discard any that are chipped or damaged.
✔ Always clamp the workpiece to a stable surface.
✔ Hold the router firmly when you turn it on to prevent it from twisting out of your hands.
✔ Let the motor reach full speed before starting the cut.
✔ Guide the tool into the workpiece against the direction of bit rotation.
✔ For deep cuts, make several passes, increasing the cutting depth gradually with each pass, rather than trying to reach your final depth in a single pass.
✔ Turn off the router as soon as the pass is done; wait until the bit has stopped spinning before setting the tool down.

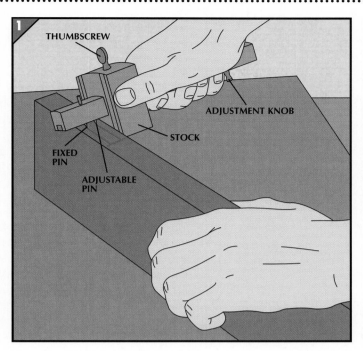

1. Marking the mortise.

◆ Mark both ends of the mortise with a combination square.

◆ Adjust a mortise gauge so the gap between its fixed and adjustable pins is the same as the width of the mortise you need: Loosen the knob on the handle, slide the adjustable pin to the correct position, and tighten the knob. To position the mortise outline at the desired location on the workpiece, loosen the thumbscrew on the stock and slide the stock along the handle so the gap between it and the adjustable pin equals the gap between the edge of the workpiece and the mortise location. Tighten the thumbscrew.

◆ Guide the gauge along the surface of the workpiece while holding the gauge's stock flush against the edge; the pins will scribe the sides of the mortise outline in the wood *(left)*.

2. Creating the mortise.

◆ Mark a line through the center of the outline to help you align the bit.

◆ Fasten the workpiece in hand-screw clamps, then secure the assembly to a work surface with the mortise outline facing up.

◆ Install a bit of a diameter equal to the width of the mortise in an electric drill; add a stop collar or wrap masking tape around the bit at the depth you want the mortise.

◆ With the bit directly over the centerline, hold the drill with both hands to keep it perpendicular to the edge of the board and bore a hole at each end of the mortise outline, stopping when the stop collar or the tape contact the board. Then make a series of overlapping holes *(near right)* to remove as much waste as possible.

◆ Square the mortise with a bevel-edged chisel, keeping the blade perfectly vertical and its beveled edge facing the inside of the mortise *(far right)*. Use a chisel with a blade equal to the mortise width to clean up the ends.

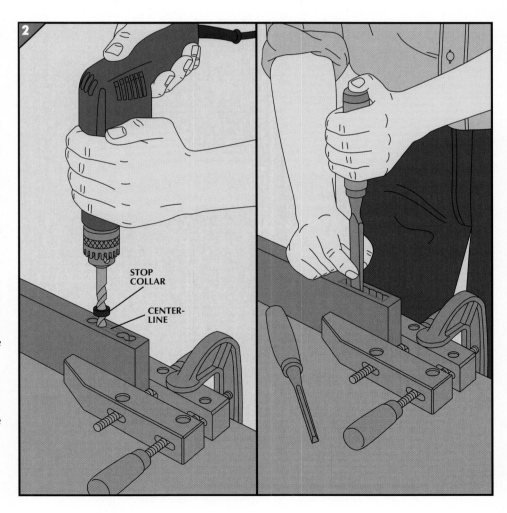

USING A PLUNGE ROUTER

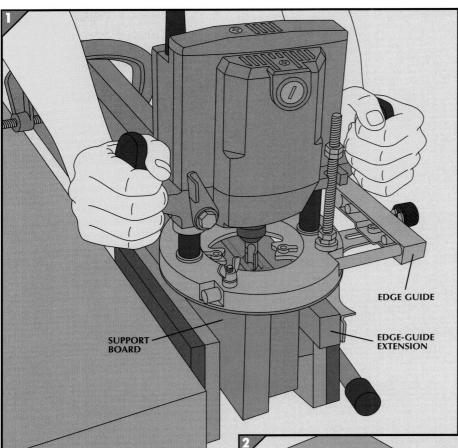

SUPPORT BOARD

EDGE GUIDE

EDGE-GUIDE EXTENSION

1. Routing out the mortise.
◆ Outline the mortise on the edge of the workpiece *(page 59, Step 1)*.
◆ Secure the board edge-up in a vise along with a support board to provide more bearing surface for the router's base plate; make sure the top surfaces of the two boards are level.
◆ Install a mortising bit the same diameter as the width of the mortise in a plunge router, then set the desired depth of cut.
◆ Attach a wooden extension to the fence of a commercial edge guide; fasten the guide to the router's base plate.
◆ Center the bit over the mortise outline and adjust the extension so that it rests flush against the workpiece. Holding the router firmly, plunge the bit into the workpiece at one end of the mortise *(left)*, then feed the cutter to the other end.

2. Squaring the corners.
◆ Clamp the stock to a work surface.
◆ To square the rounded corners of the mortise, use a beveled-edge chisel with a blade width equal to that of the mortise. Holding the tool perfectly vertical with the bevel facing the waste, strike it with a mallet *(right)*. Repeat the procedure on the other end of the mortise.

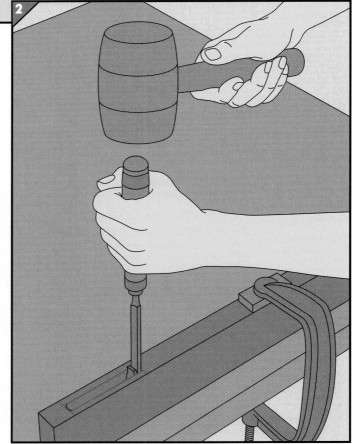

WORKING WITH A DRILL PRESS

1. Setting up the mortising attachment.

A mortising attachment consists of a drill bit surrounded by a four-sided hollow mortise chisel that squares the hole cut by the bit. Choose a chisel equal in size to the width of mortise you are boring.

◆ Install the attachment on the drill press.

◆ Check the adjustment of the chisel on a scrap board the same width and thickness as the workpiece: Position the board against the fence of the mortising attachment, then set the hold-down arm and rods to steady the piece while allowing it to slide along the fence.

◆ Bore a shallow hole in the board *(Step 2)*, then turn the piece of wood around end-to-end and make a second cut next to the first. If the cuts aren't aligned, shift the fence by one-half the amount that the cuts are misaligned and repeat the test *(right)*. (For the sake of clarity, the hold-down arm is shown raised.)

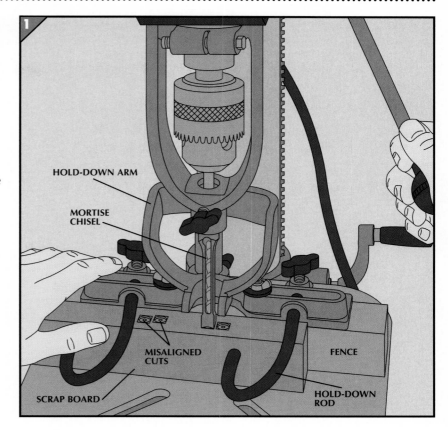

HOLD-DOWN ARM

MORTISE CHISEL

MISALIGNED CUTS

FENCE

SCRAP BOARD

HOLD-DOWN ROD

2. Boring the mortise.

◆ Set the drilling depth to the desired depth of the mortise.

◆ With the mortise outline centered under the chisel, set the hold-down arm and rods to steady the workpiece against the fence as you did in Step 1.

◆ Make a cut at each end of the outline, then follow the sequence shown *(inset)* to make a series of staggered cuts to complete the mortise *(left)*.

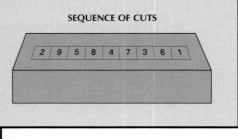

SEQUENCE OF CUTS

2 9 5 8 4 7 3 6 1

Techniques for Shaping Wood

Wood is molded with a variety of tools and methods. For smoothing surfaces, you can use traditional hand tools such as planes and spokeshaves. Handsaws and chisels are best for cutting notches. For rabbets and dadoes, the radial-arm saw and router are unsurpassed; and when mounted in a table, the router becomes a stationary tool capable of shaping trim and moldings.

Planing a board's edge →

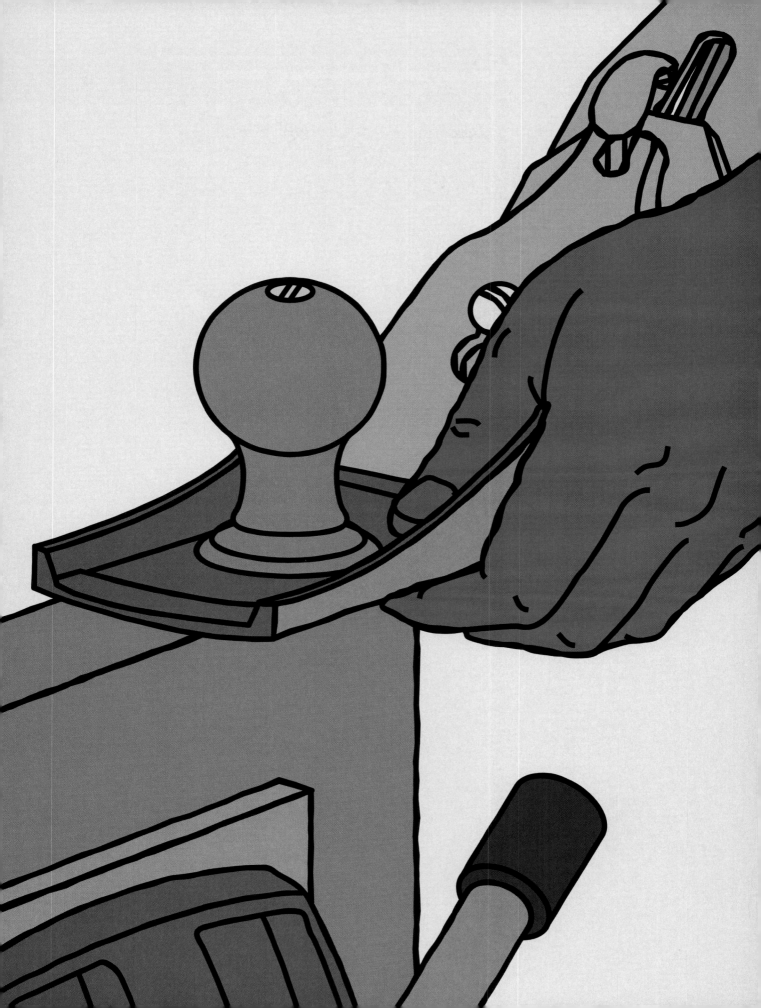

For trimming and smoothing wood, no tool is more accurate than a hand plane with a razor-sharp edge. However, the tool's major shortcoming is its reliance on muscle power. For big jobs, you may want to ease the work with a portable planer; use a belt sander to fine-tune surfaces and eliminate flaws.

Hand Planes: These tools come in a variety of sizes and models. A 14-inch jack plane is a good, all-purpose type. All bench planes have the same basic design: The blade, or iron, is mounted bevel-side down, and protrudes through a slot—called a mouth—in the sole of the plane. To remove the blade for sharpening, the tool must be taken apart. The blade can then be adjusted during re-assembly *(below and pages 65-66)*.

Smaller, one-hand block planes are best for light trimming jobs and for smoothing end grain. Adjust the blade for different woods *(page 69)*.

Whatever plane you use, cut with the grain wherever possible to avoid tearing the wood fiber; if the grain changes direction along the board, adapt your stroke to accommodate the differences.

Power Planers and Sanders: Portable planers shear away wood fiber rapidly *(page 70)*. Although these tools can cut either across or against the grain, work with the grain for best results. Belt sanders are used with the wood grain as well *(page 71)*. For reducing the thickness of boards or smoothing a wide surface quickly, choose a stationary planer *(page 71)*.

 TOOLS

Bench plane
Screwdriver
Vise
C-clamps

Hammer
Block plane
Portable planer
Belt sander

 MATERIALS

Plywood ($\frac{3}{4}$")

Scrap wood
Common nails
Sanding belt

 SAFETY TIPS

Put on goggles when operating a power tool; add a dust mask when smoothing wood with a belt sander.

ASSEMBLING AND ADJUSTING A BENCH PLANE

1. Joining the irons.
◆ Thread the cap screw lightly into the cap iron.
◆ Holding the iron bevel side out at a right angle to the cap iron, slip the head of the cap screw through the hole at the end of the slot in the iron, and slide the cap iron about halfway along the slot *(right)*.
◆ Being careful not to scrape the cap iron across the iron's cutting edge, rotate the cap iron until the edges of the two irons align.
◆ Slide the cap iron forward gently until the front of its nose is about $\frac{1}{16}$ inch behind the iron's cutting edge.
◆ Tighten the cap screw by hand, then give it an additional quarter turn with a screwdriver.

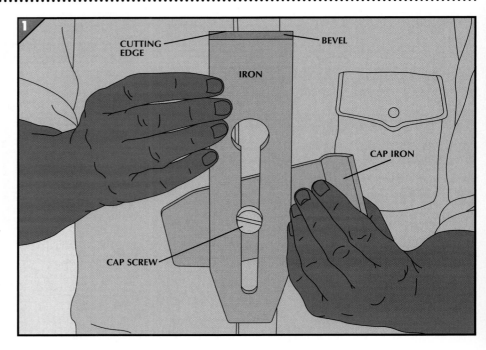

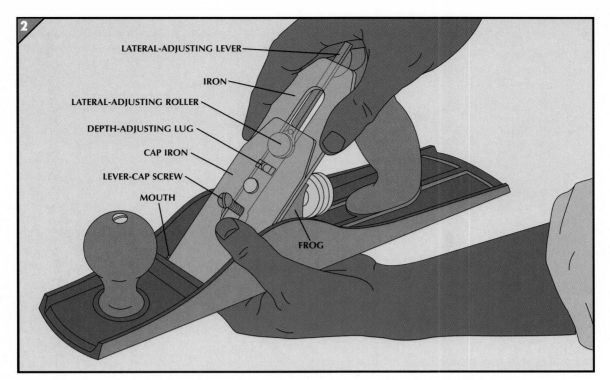

LATERAL-ADJUSTING LEVER
IRON
LATERAL-ADJUSTING ROLLER
DEPTH-ADJUSTING LUG
CAP IRON
LEVER-CAP SCREW
MOUTH
FROG

2. Installing the irons.

◆ Insert the cutting edge into the mouth of the plane as you fit the irons over the lever-cap screw, and lay the irons on the frog so the top of the depth-adjusting lug fits into the window in the cap iron and the lateral-adjusting roller fits into the iron's slot *(above)*.

◆ Place the lever cap *(page 66, Step 4)* on the irons, then slide it down until the narrow portion of its hole fits around the lever-cap screw, and snap the cam down with moderate thumb pressure. If the cam does not snap down properly, release it and loosen the lever-cap screw to decrease tension or tighten it to increase tension.

3. Setting the blade depth.

◆ Hold the plane upright, with the heel—the back end—resting on a light-colored surface and the sole facing away from you.

◆ Sighting down the sole, turn the depth-adjusting nut until the blade barely protrudes from the mouth about $\frac{1}{32}$ inch *(right)*; if the blade sticks out farther at one side of the mouth than at the other, even it with the lateral-adjusting lever. On the final adjustment of the nut, be sure that the direction of the turn moves the blade deeper through the mouth, rather than shallower—otherwise the blade will slide back slightly during your first stroke due to the small amount of play present in the adjustment mechanism.

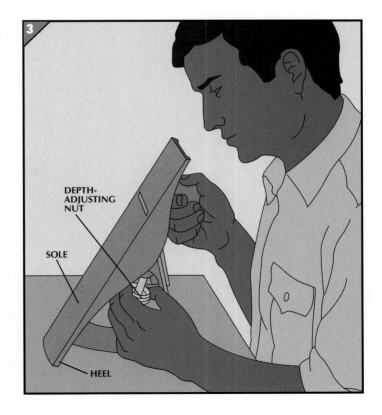

DEPTH-ADJUSTING NUT
SOLE
HEEL

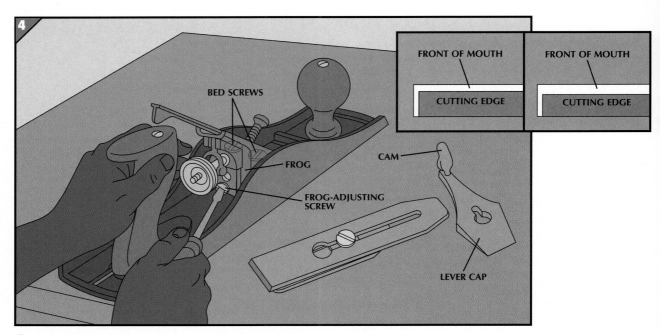

BED SCREWS

FROG

FROG-ADJUSTING SCREW

CAM

LEVER CAP

FRONT OF MOUTH

CUTTING EDGE

FRONT OF MOUTH

CUTTING EDGE

4. Adjusting the mouth.

◆ Turn the sole toward you to check the mouth opening. For easy-to-cut wood—softwoods such as pine—a wide opening is best *(inset, left)*; for harder material—hardwoods like oak— you need a narrow opening *(inset, right)*.

◆ To either widen or narrow the opening, remove the lever cap and the irons, exposing the bed screws in the frog. Loosen the screws, then retract or advance the frog-adjusting screw *(above)*—usually only a slight adjustment is needed.

◆ Reassemble the plane *(Step 2)*, check the mouth opening again, and plane a piece of scrap wood. If the shavings are not paper thin, readjust the mouth until they are.

WORKING WITH THE TOOL

Planing an edge.

◆ Fasten the board in a vise, protecting the clamped surface with wood pads.

◆ With the toe—the front end—of the plane set squarely on the end of the board, place one hand on the rear handle of the plane. Curl your other hand around the side of the tool so your thumb rests near the knob, your fingertips touch the sole just ahead of the blade, and the backs of your fingers brush the face of the board under the plane. If the wood is splintery, place your hand on the knob of the plane, rather than under it.

◆ Start the first pass with more pressure on the toe than on the heel *(right)*. Then, allow pressure to shift so it is even by the middle of the pass.

◆ When the blade reaches the opposite end of the board, apply slightly more pressure on the heel to ensure that the sole runs flat on the surface.

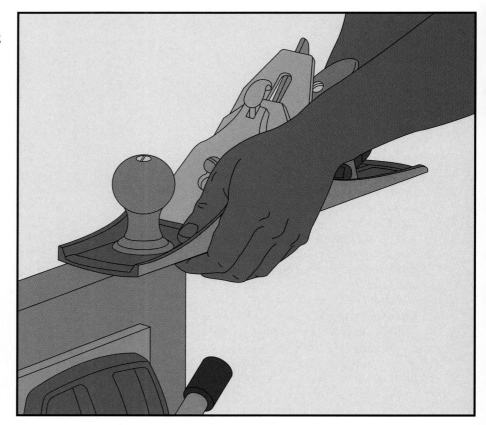

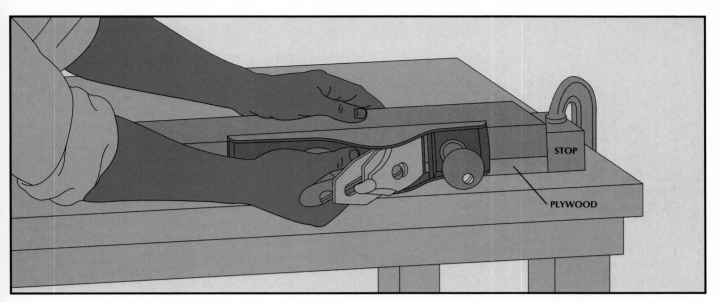

STOP

PLYWOOD

Using a shooting board.

◆ To plane the edge of a board so it is exactly perpendicular to its face, set a piece of plywood on the bench and place the board on top so its edge overlaps the edge of the plywood by about $\frac{1}{8}$ inch.

◆ With a C-clamp, secure a wood block to the workbench at the end of the plywood to serve as a stop, and butt both boards against the stop.

◆ Holding the board and plywood in place with one hand,

lay the plane on its side and shave the edge of the board toward the stop until it is flush with the plywood *(above)*. If you find it difficult to hold the board steady, place a second stop at the other end of the board.

To shoot multiple boards in succession, build a permanent shooting board similar to the mitered one on page 74, but substitute a perpendicular stop on one end for the mitered stop.

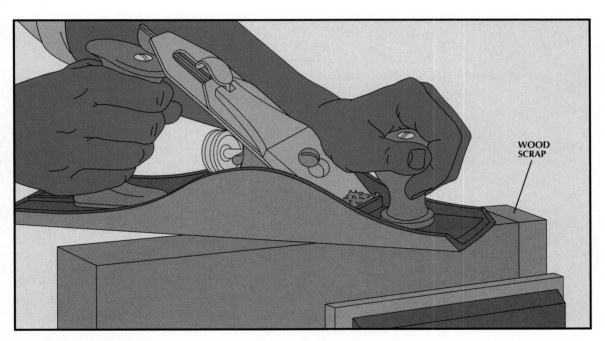

WOOD
SCRAP

Planing end grain.

◆ Protecting its faces with wood pads, clamp the board end up in a vise along with a wood scrap as wide as the board is thick to extend the planing surface beyond the edge of the board. If possible, clamp the scrap to the board so the planing action cannot cause the two to separate.

◆ Set the plane flat on the end of the board at about a 30-degree angle across it, and shave the

end grain from one edge to the other *(above)*, continuing your strokes onto the scrap.

If you cannot fit a wood scrap into the vise, start at one end and plane about three-quarters of the surface; then, after a few passes, reverse direction, starting the strokes at the opposite end of the board and planing toward, but not over, the portion you already smoothed.

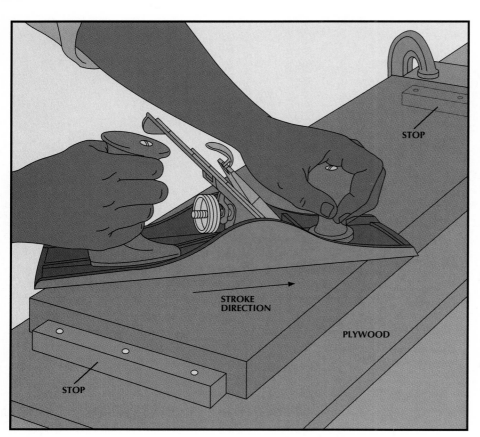

Leveling and smoothing a face.
◆ Place the board on a piece of $\frac{3}{4}$-inch plywood, butt a wood block against each end of the board as a stop, and fasten the stops in place with common nails. Clamp the plywood to the workbench.
◆ Plane the board in two stages, first for leveling, then for smoothing. To level the face, hold the plane at an angle of about 45 degrees to the wood's grain direction, and shave the surface with straight, slightly overlapping strokes with the edge of the blade at right angles to the direction of the strokes *(left)*. To smooth the face, take the plane apart and sharpen the cutting edge. Reassemble the plane *(pages 64-66, Steps 1-4)* and continue shaving the surface with straight strokes parallel to the grain.

STOP

STROKE DIRECTION

PLYWOOD

STOP

TRICKS OF THE TRADE

Checking the Flatness of a Board

You can use a plane to determine whether a surface is flat. Simply tip the tool onto the corner formed by the sole and one side *(right)* and hold it on the surface at several points. If the corner rests flush along its entire length—with no gaps between it and the board—the surface is flat. Any spots with gaps require further leveling, as described above.

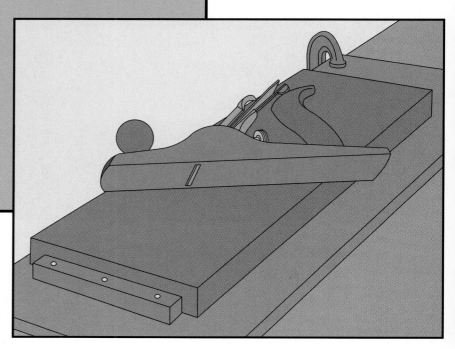

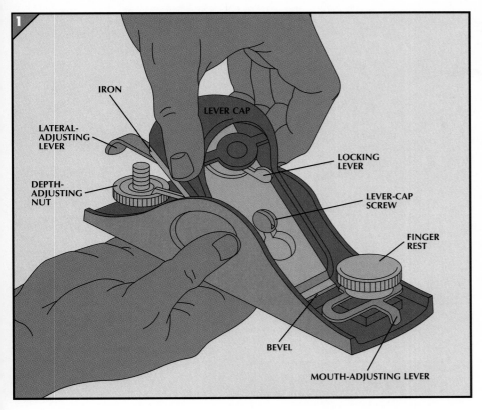

IRON

LEVER CAP

LATERAL-
ADJUSTING
LEVER

LOCKING
LEVER

DEPTH-
ADJUSTING
NUT

LEVER-CAP
SCREW

FINGER
REST

BEVEL

MOUTH-ADJUSTING LEVER

1. Adjusting the plane.

◆ Holding the plane in one hand, use the other to insert the iron, bevel up, then fit the lever cap over the iron *(left)*, and tighten the locking lever.

◆ Turn the plane upside down so you can sight along the sole. Set the depth of the blade with the depth-adjusting nut and align the blade with the lateral-adjusting lever so that it is parallel to the sole.

◆ For trimming edges on easy-to-cut woods such as pine, loosen the finger-rest screw and shift the mouth-adjusting lever to open the mouth to about $\frac{1}{16}$ inch; for end grain, harder-to-cut woods like oak, and plywood, close the mouth to about   inch.

2. Trimming the wood.

◆ Clamp the board in a vise so the surface to be trimmed faces up.

◆ Hold the plane in one hand with your palm on the lever cap, your index finger on the finger rest, and your thumb and remaining fingers on the sides.

◆ Begin each stroke with slightly more pressure on the toe and finish it with slightly more pressure on the heel *(right)*. If the plane vibrates and is hard to push, reduce the depth of cut.

On end grain and plywood, the plane should produce small chips of wood rather than shavings.

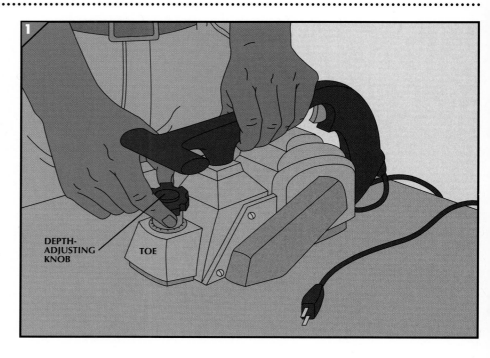

1. Setting the depth of cut.
◆ With the power cord unplugged, turn the depth-adjusting knob to raise or lower the toe of the planer *(right)*. With most models, the maximum recommended cutting depth is about $\frac{1}{16}$ inch—suitable for rough wood. A full turn of the knob raises or lowers the toe about $\frac{1}{16}$ inch.
◆ Test the cutting depth by making a few trial passes on scrap wood; change the adjustment if necessary.

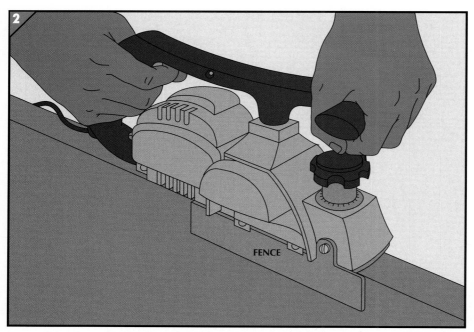

2. Planing an edge.
◆ Clamp the work so the edge to be planed faces up. If you want the edge to be exactly perpendicular to the face, attach the fence supplied with the tool to the planer.
◆ Gripping both handles of the planer firmly, set the toe on the edge of the board at one end with the blade clear of the wood and the fence flat against the board's face.
◆ Start the motor, let it reach maximum speed, and start the cut, applying more pressure at the beginning. Move the plane forward steadily to complete the cut *(left)*; for a smooth cut, guide the planer slowly.

Portable Planer Safety

✔ Fasten the work securely—in a vise, with clamps, or between stops on a workbench as shown on page 68 *(top)*.
✔ Keep both hands on the planer handle at all times. Never curl your fingers under the sole to guide the plane.
✔ Wait until the motor has stopped completely before setting the plane down at the end of a cut.

BELT-SANDING A BOARD

STOP

STOP

Smoothing with a belt sander.

◆ Fit the sander with a sanding belt that is appropriate for the job—grits range from 60 for leveling deep scratches in wood to 600 for sanding between coats of lacquer finish. To ensure that the sander remains flat on the surface you can fit it into a sanding frame *(photograph)*.

◆ Place the panel on your workbench and clamp a stop at each end to hold it in place.

◆ Starting at one corner of the panel, set the tool flat on the surface parallel to the grain, and move it forward immediately; once it reaches the opposite end, shift the sander over by half the width of the belt and pull the tool back toward you.

◆ Continue sanding back and forth, following a U-shaped pattern *(left)*.

A STATIONARY PLANER

A stationary planer, such as the benchtop model shown below, is the ideal machine for smoothing rough stock, planing lumber, or reducing the thickness of a board uniformly. The board is fed into the machine at one end, where it is pressed down flat on the table. Above the board a cutterhead—fitted with up to three knives—planes wood from the board, producing a smooth surface that is parallel with the opposite face.

When using a planer, always feed stock into it following the direction of grain. Although the maximum depth of cut for most machines is $\frac{1}{8}$ inch, limit each pass to $\frac{1}{16}$ inch and make multiple passes to remove the desired amount of wood.

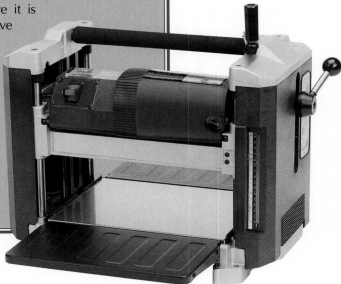

Shaping to Angles and Curves

Some jobs require that you shape boards to angles or curves. A door edge, for example, is beveled across its entire width so the door will close easily. In other instances, you may need to produce a curve or bend. To achieve these shapes, you will need special techniques and, in some cases, special tools.

Tools for Bevels and Curves: To cut bevels or relieve sharp-edged corners, use a bench plane to shape the corner into a chamfer (below). A decorative variant of the chamfer that runs only partway along the edge is achieved with a spokeshave (opposite); this tool can also be substituted for a rasp or sandpaper to finish curved edges. To smooth the end of a board cut at a 45-degree angle, a shop-made miter shooting board will serve as a guide for a bench plane (page 74).

Bending Wood: Bowing a board around a curve can be done by making a series of cuts or kerfs in the back of the board to allow it to bend (pages 75-76). For this technique to succeed, use a board less than 1 inch thick; have thicker wood bent by a professional. In addition, select straight, clear lumber, free of knots and cracks. Woods with long fibers—oak, pine, and fir, for example—can be bent easily with kerfing; woods with shorter fibers such as cherry and maple are stiffer and cannot be bent into tight curves.

To conceal the kerfs along the top, fill them with wood filler and sand the edge. If the curve is fairly shallow, you can use plain stock and cover the cut edge with quarter-round or ogee molding, which is flexible enough to be bent without any kerfing.

 TOOLS

Vise	Circular saw
T-bevel	Straightedge
Mortise gauge	Tape measure
Bench plane	Radial-arm saw
Spokeshave	Electric drill
Screwdriver	Hammer

 **MATERIALS**

Plywood ($\frac{3}{4}$")	Scrap wood
Wood screws ($1\frac{1}{4}$" No. 6)	Finishing nails ($1\frac{1}{4}$")

🔨 **SAFETY TIPS**

Goggles prevent injury to eyes when you are operating a power tool or when driving nails.

CHAMFERING WITH A BENCH PLANE

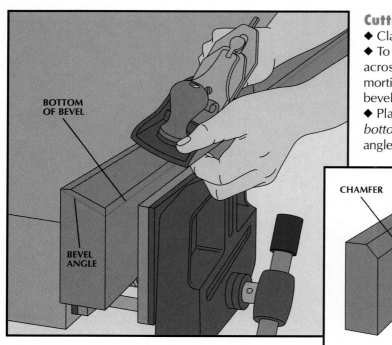

BOTTOM OF BEVEL

BEVEL ANGLE

CHAMFER

Cutting bevels and chamfers.
◆ Clamp the board in a vise.
◆ To cut a bevel along the edge, mark the desired angle across the end of the board with a T-bevel. Then, with a mortise gauge (page 59), scribe a line for the bottom of the bevel along the face of the board.
◆ Plane the bevel as you would a square edge (page 66, bottom), but tilt the sole of the plane parallel to the bevel-angle line (left). As the plane nears the corner of the board at one face and the line for the bottom of the bevel on the opposite face, adjust the angle of the sole precisely to reach both simultaneously.

◆ To flatten a sharp corner over its full length into a chamfer (inset), mark the angle—usually 45 degrees—on the end of the board and scribe matching lines on the face and edge.
◆ Plane the chamfer as you would to make a bevel.

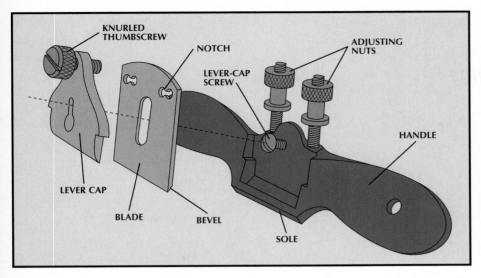

KNURLED THUMBSCREW

NOTCH

LEVER-CAP SCREW

ADJUSTING NUTS

HANDLE

LEVER CAP

BLADE

BEVEL

SOLE

Anatomy of a spokeshave.

The tool's short sole—flat-bottomed for straight and convex shapes or rounded for concave ones—allows it to plane curved surfaces. The blade is mounted bevel side down; its depth and angle are set with flanged adjusting nuts set in notches in the blade. The blade is held down by the lever cap, which is tightened by a knurled thumbscrew that presses against the top of the blade. To adjust the blade, snug up the lever-cap screw, turn the adjusting nuts until the cutting edge just projects below the sole, then hand-tighten the thumbscrew.

Cutting a stopped chamfer.

◆ Mark the ends of the chamfer with a pencil. Then, with a mortise gauge *(page 59)*, outline the sides of the chamfer on the edge and face of the board.

◆ Set a flat-bottomed spokeshave on the mark at one end, and, with the handles tilted 45 degrees from the horizontal, push the tool forward with the grain to a point $\frac{1}{8}$ inch from the other end.

◆ Continue shaving the corner *(right)* and, after every two or three passes, make a short cut at the far end of the chamfer to pare away the shavings.

◆ Once you've cut the chamfer down to the marked lines, shave the far end to a smooth, gradual curve that matches the one at the near end.

Smoothing a curve.

◆ Clamp the board in a vise so the spokeshave will be cutting in the same direction as the wood grain.

◆ With a round-bottomed spokeshave for the concave curve shown—or a flat-bottomed model for a convex curve—set the tool at the top of the curve and push it slowly to the bottom *(left)*.

◆ Reverse direction and push the spokeshave down from the other side of the curve; work back and forth until the surface is smooth. Do not push the spokeshave uphill against the wood grain; it will gouge and chip the surface.

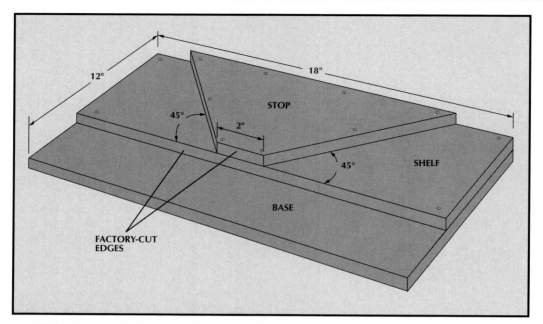

Building the shooting board.

Designed to assist in accurate planing at an angle, this jig is made from $\frac{3}{4}$-inch plywood and consists of a 9- by 18-inch shelf and and a 9-inch-wide trapezoidal stop atop a 12- by 18-inch base. The straight, factory-cut edge of the plywood is used for the side of the shelf that is stepped back from the base. The stop also has the factory-cut edge at the front; and its ends are cut to form two opposing 45-degree angles about 2 inches apart. The parts are fastened together with $1\frac{1}{4}$-inch No. 6 wood screws.

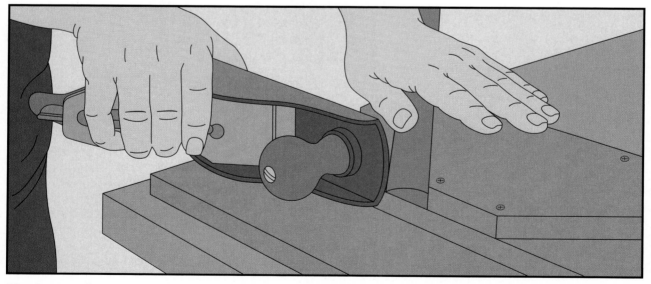

Planing a miter.

◆ Hold the workpiece firmly against one end of the stop, with its end about $\frac{1}{32}$ inch beyond the edge of the stop.
◆ Rest a bench plane on its side against the shelf with its toe against the miter (above) and slide the tool forward repeatedly, starting each stroke with the toe against the miter and stopping it when the blade passes the miter—planing farther will cut into the stop and ruin its straight edge.

◆ As you shave the workpiece, move it forward slightly so it always extends $\frac{1}{32}$ inch beyond the stop. If the plane becomes hard to push, rub paraffin on the shooting board and the side of the plane.

1. Marking the spring lines.

Where a curved board will join a straight section—as in the case of the baseboard shown here—you need to find where the curve begins. This point is called the spring line.

◆ Hold a straightedge against the straight section of the wall with its end projecting past the beginning of the curve *(right)*. Mark the first point where no space can be seen between the straightedge and the wall.

◆ Mark the spring line in the same way at the other end of the curve.

SPRING LINE

2. Measuring the curve.

◆ With a flexible tape measure, find the distance between the spring lines *(above)*.

◆ Transfer the measurement to the board you will bend, add 6 inches at each end, and cut the board.

3. Kerfing the board.

◆ Mark the fence of a radial-arm saw $\frac{1}{2}$ inch from the right side of the blade and set the blade's cutting depth $\frac{1}{8}$ inch above the saw table.

◆ Cut a kerf across the width of a 2-foot-long wood scrap of the same width and thickness as the board to be bent.

◆ Slide the scrap along the fence to align the kerf with the mark on the fence and make another cut. Continue sawing kerfs at $\frac{1}{2}$-inch intervals across the scrap.

◆ Bend the scrap around a section of the curve to test its flexibility. If you hear cracking as you bend the wood or if you need to strain to bend it, increase the saw's blade depth slightly and kerf another scrap piece, decreasing the space between cuts by $\frac{1}{8}$ inch. Repeat the test and if necessary adjust the saw to prepare another scrap—provided you leave $\frac{1}{16}$ inch of uncut wood on the back of the board and space the kerfs at least $\frac{1}{8}$ inch apart. Once you have a scrap piece that bends easily, kerf the board to be bent using the same settings on the saw (right), starting and stopping the cuts at the spring lines on the board.

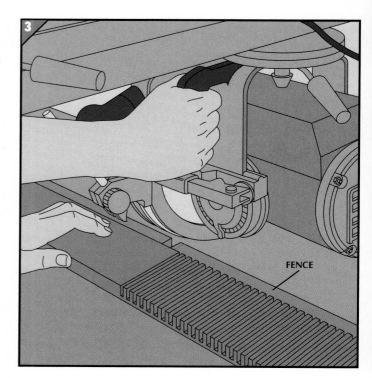

FENCE

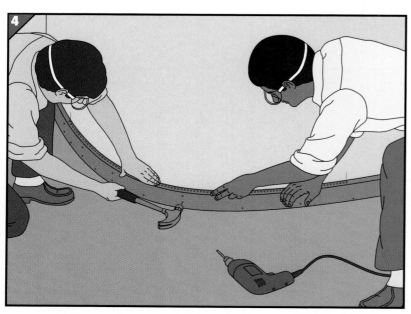

4. Fastening the board in place.

◆ With a helper holding the board in position so the first and last kerfs in the board align with the spring lines on the wall, drill a pilot hole for a finishing nail $1\frac{1}{2}$ times longer than the stock thickness through the board near one end.

◆ Drive a nail into the hole to hold the end of the board in place.

◆ Drill additional pilot holes in pairs at 8-inch intervals along the board to the opposite end.

◆ Drive a nail into each pilot hole (left).

BENDABLE PLYWOOD

. . . .

Available at lumberyards under a variety of trade names, bendable plywood is a three-ply sheet, typically between $\frac{1}{8}$ and $\frac{3}{8}$ inch thick. It features a flexible inner core sandwiched between two outer layers with parallel grain (inset), and is useful in any situation where a curved panel is required.

Cutting Out Notches

Notches are often required in studs and joists to accommodate pipes and electrical cables. A reciprocating saw *(page 79, bottom)* is an excellent tool for the job, but hand tools can also be used *(below and page 78)*—especially where space is limited. The ideal chopping tools are chisels with $\frac{3}{4}$- to $1\frac{1}{2}$-inch beveled blades and steel-capped handles strong enough to be hit with a hammer.

Meeting Code Requirements:
Consider the placement of a recess in a stud or joist carefully before making any cuts. Cutting into a framing member weakens it, and a notch in a board that supports weight—a stud in a bearing wall,

for example—must conform to the building code. Check the code before cutting a notch, but keep in mind that it may be difficult to satisfy the requirements literally. For instance, the code may prohibit a notch larger than 2 inches square. Where you need to cut a notch to fit a $2\frac{1}{2}$-inch pipe, you might be permitted to cut a larger notch if you reinforce the stud. In most cases, a kickplate—a small steel plate screwed to the board over the notch to protect the pipe or cable from nails—will meet code requirements *(page 78, bottom)*. If not, notch larger steel plates into the stud following the same method you would use for a kickplate.

 TOOLS

Wood chisel	Utility knife
Hammer	Sawhorses
Circular saw	Handsaw
Vise	

 SAFETY TIPS

Put on goggles when chiseling or when operating a power tool.

Chopping a V notch.
◆ Hold the tip of a chisel on the surface at a 45-degree angle, with the bevel toward the middle of the notch you wish to cut, and with a hammer, drive the blade into the wood, forming one side of the V.
◆ Reverse the position of the chisel to form the second side of the notch and with the bevel toward the bottom of the first cut, strike the chisel again *(right)*.

Cutting a deep notch in an edge.

◆ Set the blade of a circular saw to the depth of the notch and make two cuts across the edge of the board, outlining the notch.

◆ With a hammer, strike the wood between the saw cuts to knock out the waste *(right)*.

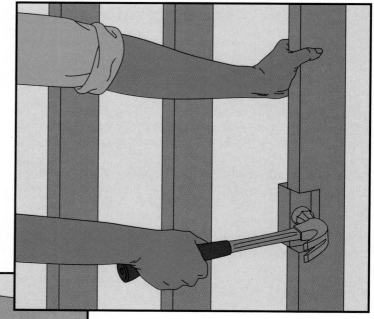

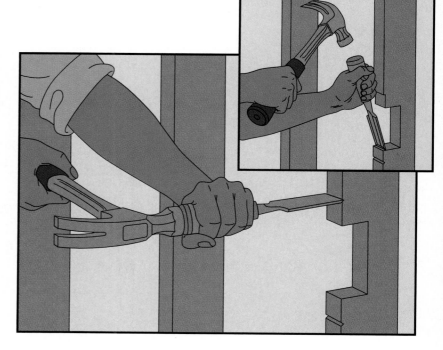

Notching a board face.

◆ With a circular saw set to the depth of the notch, make parallel cuts across the face at each side of the notch and at $\frac{1}{4}$-inch intervals in between.

◆ Clamp the board in a vise so the notch clears the jaws.

◆ To remove the waste wood, hold a chisel vertically at one corner of the notch, bevel facing the waste, and strike the handle with a hammer. Clear the remaining waste in the same way *(left)*.

Mortising a notch for a kickplate.

◆ Cut the notch in an edge of the board, then position a steel kickplate over the notch and score the wood at the ends of the kickplate using a utility knife.

◆ Hold a chisel horizontally with the tip of the blade on one scored line and the bevel facing the notch, and tap the chisel $\frac{1}{8}$ inch deep into the wood. Repeat at the other scored line *(right)*.

◆ Set the chisel $\frac{1}{8}$ inch inside each notch, bevel facing outward, and drive it into the end of the recess, paring out the waste wood to form a shallow mortise for the kickplate on each side of the notch *(inset)*.

SAW CUT

Making a shallow end notch.
◆ Clamp the board in a vise and outline the notch on the edge, face, and end of the board.
◆ With a circular saw set to the depth of the notch, cut across the edge of the board at the line.
◆ Hold a chisel horizontally with its blade on the line on the board's end and the bevel facing the waste, and drive the chisel toward the saw cut to remove the waste *(left)*.

Sawing a deep end notch.
◆ Where the depth of a notch exceeds the maximum depth of cut of your circular saw, outline the notch, secure the board on sawhorses, then use the saw to cut along the marks on the face as far as the inner corner of the notch.
◆ To complete the cuts to the corner, slide a handsaw into each circular-saw kerf and, holding the blade vertically, saw to the corner *(right)*.

CIRCULAR-SAW KERFS

A VERSATILE SAW

In situations where space permits, a reciprocating saw is a good tool for cutting notches in studs and joists. With interchangeable blades in lengths up to 6 inches, the saw will cut wood as well as plastic, wallboard, masonry, and metal. In some models, the blade can also be mounted upside down for making flush cuts in hard-to-reach spots. And like a saber saw, a reciprocating saw can make plunge cuts without first drilling a starter hole *(page 38)*.

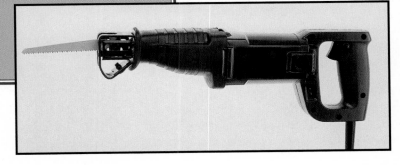

Plowing Dadoes and Rabbets

The traditional way to make a strong, gap-proof joint between boards is with an interlocking dado and rabbet or an overlapping rabbet. A rabbet is a step cut into the edge or end of a board. A dado is a rectangular channel cut across a board—a channel along the length is usually termed a groove. Rabbets and dadoes can be formed with a saw and chisel, but you can get the job done more quickly—and accurately—with a router *(below and pages 81-83)* or a radial-arm saw *(page 84).*

Working by Hand: To rabbet a board with a handsaw, make two cuts at right angles to each other along the edge. Produce a dado by making several saw cuts spaced as close as possible to one another within the area to be channeled, then chiseling out the waste wood.

The Router: To make router cuts in a perfectly straight line, you need a guide. Piloted rabbeting bits have built-in ball-bearing guides that run along the edge or end of the board

as the bit cuts, keeping it from wandering off line *(opposite, top).* Straightedge guides are simple to fashion *(opposite, bottom),* or you can attach a commercial edge guide to the tool base to cut dadoes or rabbets at the desired distance from the board edge or end.

The Radial-Arm Saw: For making identical cuts quickly in many boards, the best tool is a radial-arm saw fitted with a dado head *(page 84).*

 TOOLS

Router
Piloted rabbeting
  bit
Straight bit
Edge guide

Screwdriver
C-clamps
Hammer
Circular saw
Radial-arm saw
Dado head

 **MATERIALS**

1 x 2s
Scrap wood

Lumber for jigs
Common nails
Wood screws
  (No. 8)

 SAFETY TIPS

Protect eyes with goggles when operating power tools.

Setting depth of cut.

◆ For a router with a depth scale, set the tool on the board, loosen the locking screw, and turn the motor unit clockwise until the tip of the bit contacts the wood *(right).*

◆ Set the depth scale to zero.

◆ Move the router so the bit extends beyond the edge of the board and lower the bit until the depth scale registers the desired depth—make it no deeper than $\frac{3}{8}$ inch for the first pass; for deeper cuts, lower the bit and make additional passes.

◆ Tighten the locking screw.

To adjust the bit in a router without a depth scale, mark the depth of cut on the edge of the board, then turn the motor unit to lower the bit until its tip aligns with the depth mark *(inset).*

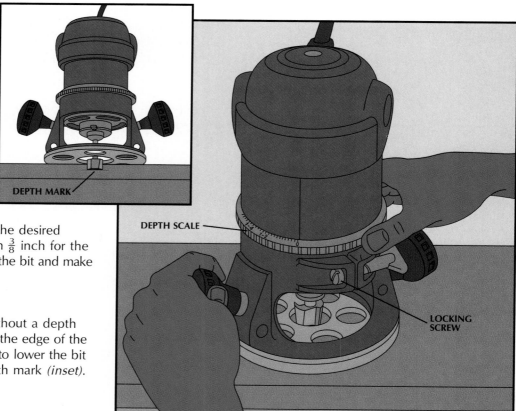

DEPTH MARK

DEPTH SCALE

LOCKING SCREW

ROUTING STRAIGHT CHANNELS WITH GUIDES

Using a piloted rabbeting bit.
◆ Clamp the board to a worktable, protecting the board's surface with wood pads.
◆ Hold the router with the bit overhanging the edge of the board about 2 inches from the end. Turn the motor on, and move the bit into the wood until the pilot bearing contacts the edge of the board.
◆ Guide the router from left to right, pressing the bearing against the edge *(right)*.
◆ Once you reach the end of the board, complete the rabbet by feeding the router from right to left through the uncut portion of the edge.

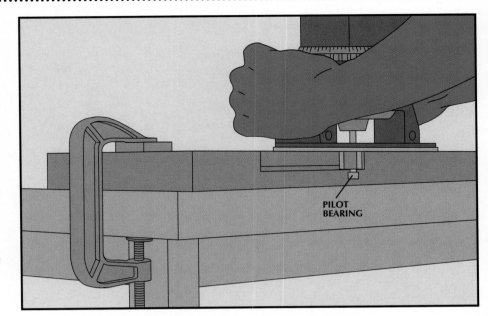

Dadoing with a shop-made guide.
◆ Outline the dado on the workpiece, then set the router down with the bit just above the surface, aligning the bit with the outline.
◆ Butt a straight piece of scrap wood as a guide against the router's base. Ensure that the guide is parallel to the outline, then clamp it to the workpiece.
◆ Starting at one end of the board, rout the dado with the tool riding along the edge guide *(above)*.

◆ For a board that is narrower than the router base, extend its surface by placing a wood scrap of equal thickness beside it. Position a guide atop the scrap in the same way you would for a wider board.
◆ Clamp the assembly to the bench *(inset)*; if necessary, stop routing and reposition the clamp to finish the cut.

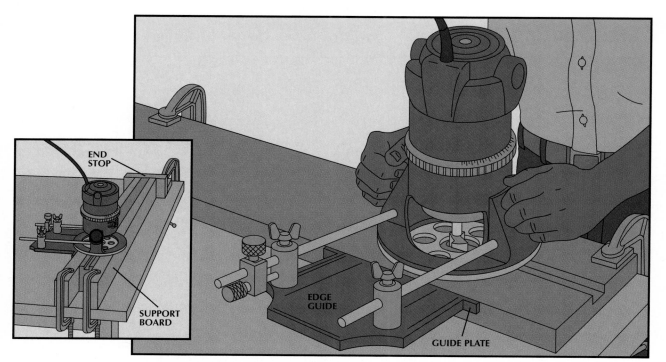

Using a commercial edge guide.
◆ Clamp the board to a work surface and outline the groove on the face near one end.
◆ Attach the edge guide to the router base, measure from one edge of the outline to the board's edge, and set the guide plate that distance from the corresponding edge of the bit.
◆ Guide the router with the plate pressing against the edge of the board (*above*).

For a board on edge, create a larger platform for the router by clamping support boards the same height as the workpiece on each side of the piece. To steady the assembly, nail two wood blocks in an L shape to form an end stop and clamp it against the opposite end of the boards. Set up the edge guide as you would for a board lying flat, but with the guide plate against the support board (*inset*).

JIGS TO SPEED REPETITIVE CUTS

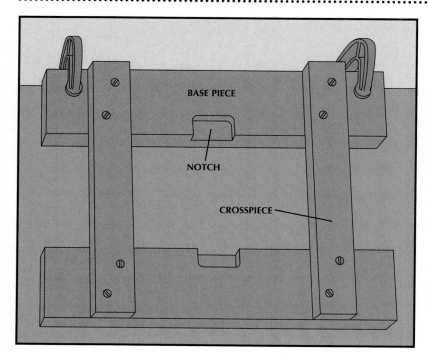

A jig for multiple straight cuts.
A simple jig can streamline the process of plowing straight dadoes or rabbets in several boards of equal dimensions.
◆ Lay two boards—each 4 inches wide, at least 2 feet long, and the same thickness as the lumber to be cut—parallel to each other, and separated by a space the same width as the boards to be cut.
◆ If you plan to make rabbets or dadoes the same width as the router bit, roughly center the router on the boards and butt two 1-by-2 crosspieces against its base plate perpendicular to the boards; then screw the crosspieces to the base. For wider rabbets or dadoes requiring more than one pass with the router, add the difference between the width of the proposed cut and the diameter of the bit to the distance between the crosspieces.
◆ Clamp the jig to a workbench, set the bit depth, and make a notch the width of the desired cut on the inner edge of each base piece; the notches will be centered between the crosspieces.

Plowing a straight dado.

◆ Outline the dado on each board to be cut and slide a board into the jig.

◆ Align the outline with the notches in the jig base and clamp the workpiece to the bench, protecting its surface with wood pads.

◆ Set the router bit in one of the notches, turn the motor on, and run the tool along one of the crosspieces to the other notch.

To complete a wide dado requiring two passes, guide the router along one crosspiece *(left)*, then push it to the other side of the notch and guide it along the second crosspiece.

Routing an angled dado.

◆ To cut dadoes at an angle across a board, prepare the jig as described opposite, but fasten the crosspieces to the base at the desired angle.

◆ Make the cut as described above for a straight dado *(right)*.

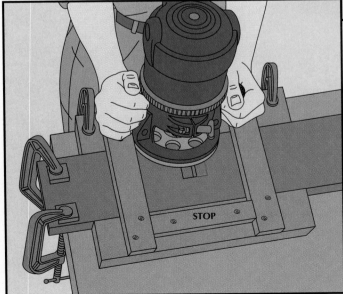

STOP

Cutting a stopped dado.

◆ To rout a dado that stops short of the edge of a board, make the jig described opposite, but notch only one of the base pieces.

◆ Screw a 1-by-2 stop to the unnotched board between the crosspieces so the distance from its edge to the end of the planned cut equals the distance from the outside edge of the bit to the rim of the router base.

◆ Make the cut as you would a straight dado. For a single pass, turn the router off when it contacts the stop. On a wide cut *(left)*, complete both passes before turning the router off.

WIDE DADOES WITH A RADIAL-ARM SAW

A dado head.

A radial-arm saw can be adapted to cut dadoes and rabbets efficiently with either of two accessories. The dado head *(near right)* replaces the regular blade with two saw blades separated by chippers and an assortment of washers. *(For the sake of clarity, the outer blade in this drawing is partially cut away.)* The width of cut—up to $\frac{13}{16}$ inch—is adjusted by assembling the blades with the appropriate chippers and washers.

Less expensive, but also less precise, the wobbler *(far right)* has two wedge-shaped washers that grip a regular blade between them, angling it on the axle so that it chews a wide path. The washers are marked so that you can adjust them for a cut as much as $\frac{13}{16}$ inch wide.

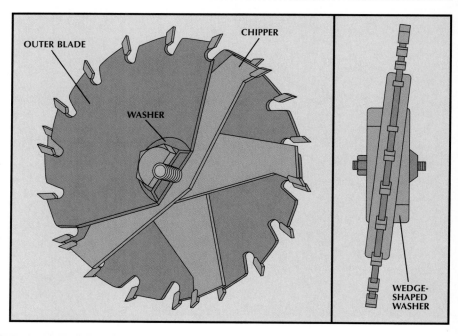

OUTER BLADE

CHIPPER

WASHER

WEDGE-SHAPED WASHER

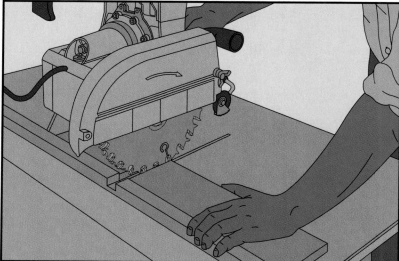

Sawing a dado.

◆ Outline the width of the dado on the face of the board to be cut.
◆ With the saw behind the fence in its crosscutting position *(page 20)*, lower the blades to the desired depth of cut and cut a kerf through the fence.
◆ Slide the yoke behind the fence, align the outline on the board with the kerf in the fence and, holding the board against the fence, pull the yoke to cut the dado *(left)*.

TRICKS OF THE TRADE

Equally Spaced Dadoes

To saw dadoes at uniform intervals along a board, cut the first one as described above, then slide the board along the fence, aligning the second dado's location with the kerf in the fence. Before making the cut, drive a screw into the fence so the head butts against the left-hand edge of the first dado. Then cut the second dado and slide the board along so the left edge of the second channel sits against the screw head. Cut the remaining dadoes the same way.

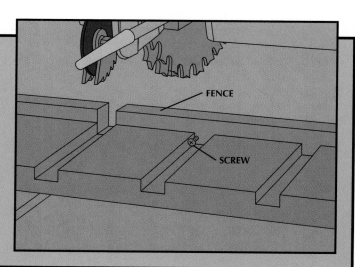

FENCE

SCREW

Fashioning Custom Molding

Although lumberyards and home centers sell many styles of moldings to trim doors and windows and form baseboards, with a router you can produce custom trim to suit your taste.

Router Bits: For shaping decorative edges or grooves, bits come in a large range of styles and sizes that can make cuts as much as $1\frac{5}{8}$ inches wide and $\frac{3}{4}$ inch deep (*below*). By combining cuts with several bits, you can duplicate or create almost any

molding shape. To check the cut that will be made by a bit or a combination of cutters, make test cuts on scrap wood at least 1 inch thick and free of knots or warping.

Stationary Routing: A small amount of trim can be made with a hand-held router, but for large quantities, convert your router into a mini-shaper by mounting it upside down in a table (*pages 86-87*). This enables you to repeat the same cut accurately on multiple boards.

Router-Table Safety: Always feed the workpiece into the bit against the direction of bit rotation. Since the router bit is exposed above the table surface, keep your hands well away from the rotating cutter and finish off any cuts along the edge of a board with a push stick. A shoe-shaped push stick is best, as this type permits you to apply downward as well as forward pressure. To make sure you can shut off the router quickly, power the tool from a switched receptacle mounted on the worktable.

TOOLS

Circular saw
Electric drill
Counterbore bit
Screwdriver
Saber saw
C-clamps
Router
Piloted edging bit
Featherboard
Push stick

MATERIALS

1 x 2, 2 x 8s
Scrap lumber
Plywood ($\frac{1}{2}$")
Wood screws (1" No. 8)
Switched receptacle
Electrical wire

SAFETY TIPS

Put on goggles when operating a power tool.

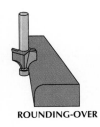
ROUNDING-OVER

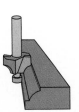
BEADING WITH TWO FLUTES

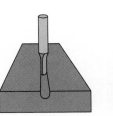
ROMAN OGEE

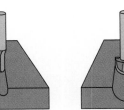
VEINING

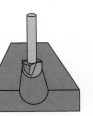
CORE BOX

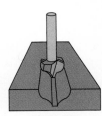
OGEE WITH TWO FLUTES

OGEE WITH TWO FILLETS

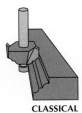
CLASSICAL

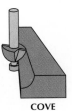
COVE

EDGING BITS

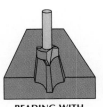
BEADING WITH TWO FLUTES

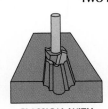
CLASSICAL WITH TWO FLUTES

GROOVING BITS

A catalog of cutters.

This selection of router bits represents only a fraction of the profiles available for forming edges and plowing grooves. Edging bits generally have ball-bearing pilot guides that ride along the side of a board to keep the router cutting straight. The width of any cut is limited by the width of the bit, but cutters can be used in combination to create wider designs;

for example, a deep cut with a core-box bit next to a shallow cut with a rounding-over bit would produce an ogee curve wider than the one that an ogee bit used alone can produce. Since the router's depth of cut is adjustable, some cutters—such as the ogee edging bit with two fillets—can produce more than one profile, depending on the depth to which the router is set.

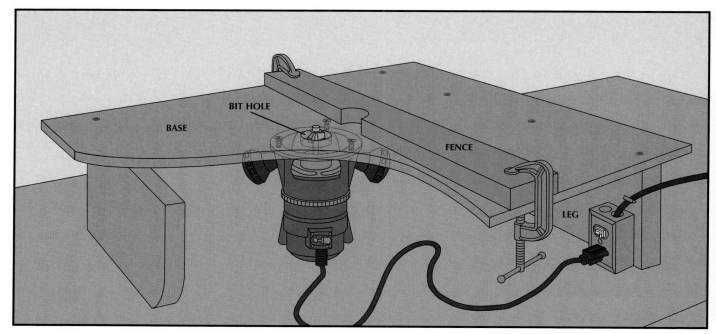

Building the router table.

◆ For the base, cut a piece of $\frac{1}{2}$-inch plywood $2\frac{1}{2}$ to 3 feet square, or no wider than a commercial fence *(box, below)* if you plan to use one.

◆ For the legs, use two boards wide enough to provide clearance for the router, such as 2-by-8s or 2-by-10s, and cut them the same length as the table.

◆ Set the base on the legs so that the base overhangs enough to fit C-clamps anywhere at its edges, then fasten it to each leg with four 1-inch No. 8 wood screws.

◆ To position the bit hole at the center of the base, mark diagonal lines from corner to corner, then at the intersection of the marks, drill a hole $\frac{1}{8}$ inch larger than the widest bit you plan to use.

◆ Remove the base from the router, center the tool over the bit hole, and mark the location of the screw holes in the base. At each mark, countersink a hole for the screws removed from the router.

◆ For the fence, cut a 1-by-2 long enough to span the base. In the middle of one edge of the fence, cut a semicircular notch the same diameter as the table's bit hole. Hold the fence to the base with C-clamps; you will then be able to reposition it to accommodate the width of each board that is being shaped.

◆ Mount a switched receptacle on one of the router-table legs and plug the router into the receptacle.

ROUTER-TABLE ACCESSORIES

Several commercial accessories can make a table-mounted router easier to use *(right)*. The fence, for example, features a vacuum attachment that draws away sawdust and wood chips. The foot switch allows you to turn the router on and off without using the tool's switch; placing the switch inside a switch guard prevents accidental startup of the tool. The variable-speed switch allows the operator to control the router's velocity, useful when using larger bits that call for reduced speed. With either the foot switch or variable-speed switch, plug the router into the accessory, then plug the accessory into a receptacle.

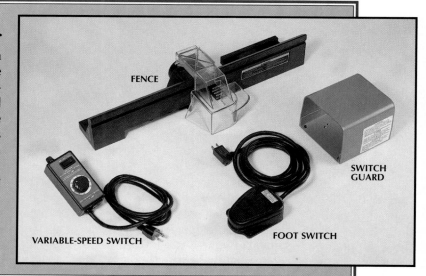

Shaping board ends.

◆ With the notch in the fence over the bit hole, align the edge of the fence with the bit's pilot guide—this will ensure that the workpiece runs along the pilot during the cut; then, clamp the fence in place.

◆ To help you feed the work across the table at a 90-degree angle to the fence, use a scrap board. Set the workpiece and scrap board on the table, clear of the bit, with their ends flush against the fence. Turn on the router, and holding the workpiece firmly against the scrap board, push both pieces along the fence into the bit *(right)*. Keep your hands well away from the bit as you pass it.

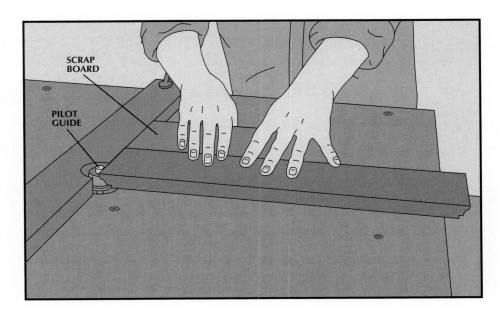

SCRAP BOARD

PILOT GUIDE

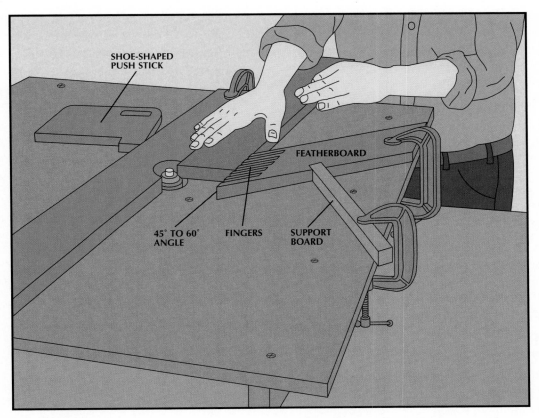

SHOE-SHAPED PUSH STICK

FEATHERBOARD

45° TO 60° ANGLE   FINGERS   SUPPORT BOARD

Routing edges.

◆ To help keep a board flush against the fence as you shape its edge, use a feather-board. Make the featherboard from a piece of hardwood, mitering one end at a 45- to 60-degree angle. Cut a series of 5-inch-long kerfs from the mitered end at $\frac{1}{8}$-inch inter-vals, creating springy fingers. Cut a notch for a support board along the long edge.

◆ Align the fence as you would for shaping board ends, then clamp the fence in place.

◆ Set the board to be shaped against the fence, then place the featherboard against the board in line with the bit, place scrap wood as a support board in the notch, and clamp both pieces to the table.

◆ Turn on the router and feed the work-piece along the fence and into the bit *(above)*. Finish the cut with a push stick to keep your hands well away from the bit.

Perfect Joints

Joinery is a subtle blend of art and engineering. Some joints are as simple as a few nails that secure two boards together; others involve elaborate interlocking parts. This chapter will show you how to master the most commonly used joints—from mechanical fasteners to the venerable mortise and tenon—and incorporate them into your woodworking projects.

Lock-nailing a miter joint →

An Arsenal of Metal Fasteners

Many joints in wood rely on metal fasteners. Although some joints are held by glue and others are shaped in interlocking parts, nails, screws, bolts, and a host of specialized steel connectors give woodworkers a fast, efficient means of joinery. Choosing the correct one for a specific job involves considering the strength needed for the joint, the possibility that it may have to be unfastened later, and the importance of its appearance. A chart summarizing the various fasteners and their uses appears on pages 92 to 93.

Nails and Screws: The most common of all fasteners, nails are quick, easy to use, and inexpensive. Like all metal fasteners, they work by friction: A driven nail displaces wood fibers, which clamp the shank of the nail tightly. Once a nail is in place, two kinds of force can dislodge it. One kind, shearing stress, is exerted at an angle perpendicular to the shank. The other, withdrawal stress, is applied parallel and opposite to the direction of entry. A nail withstands shearing better than withdrawal stress; whenever possible, drive a nail across the grain, so that the main force against it, once it is in place, is shearing force.

Screws have greater holding power than nails against withdrawal stress because their threads create greater friction with the wood fibers. Screws are also easy to remove without splintering or gouging wood.

Other Fasteners: Bolts and nuts are less commonly used than nails and screws, because both ends of the bolt must be accessible, an impossibility in many situations. However, they form exceptionally tight, strong joints between pieces that are too large for other fasteners. Some fasteners are relatively specialized: In rough construction, framing connectors secure structural members *(box, opposite)*.

NAILS, SCREWS, BOLTS, AND ANCHORS

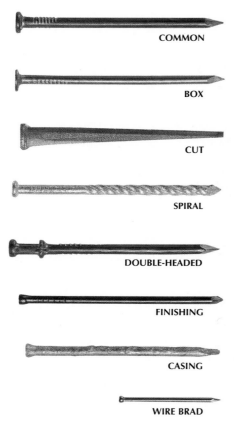

COMMON

BOX

CUT

SPIRAL

DOUBLE-HEADED

FINISHING

CASING

WIRE BRAD

Nails.
Common nails are used in general construction; box nails, almost identical, have a thinner shaft and are useful on thin boards where splitting is a danger. Common nails and box nails are used for jobs in which the appearance of the surface is not important. Both types are available with a resin coating, which heats as the nail is driven and forms an adhesive bond between the nail and the wood. When exposed, cut nails lend a rustic appearance to wood flooring. In tongue-and-groove flooring joints, spiral nails are hidden from view but tightly grip the subfloor and the joists below. Double-headed nails are designed for temporary installation, such as forms for concrete—the top heads, raised above the wood, are easy to grip to remove the nails. Finishing nails and casing nails, used in finish work, are almost interchangeable, although for heavier jobs, casing nails provide greater strength than finishing nails. Both have small heads, which can easily be driven below the surface of the wood with a nail set. The wire brad, smallest nail of all, fastens the thinnest pieces of wood.

LAG SCREW

FLAT-HEAD SCREW

ROUND-HEAD SCREW

SHEET-METAL SCREW

SINGLE-SLOT HEAD

PHILLIPS HEAD

SQUARE-DRIVE HEAD

Screws.

Screws differ in size, head shape, and slot shape. Lag screws are the largest and are used for heavy work. Their square or hexagonal heads are turned by wrenches; some have slots, and can be turned by screwdrivers as well. Lag screws are sized in inches for both length and diameter.

Standard wood screws—those with smooth shanks and slotted heads—are available in different head shapes and slot types. Flat-heads are the most common because they are easily countersunk below the wood surface and covered with putty or plugs. Round-heads generally are left exposed for decorative effect. Phillips and square-drive slots offer better control of the screwhead than the single-slot type. Standard screws are sized by diameter in gauge number and by length in inches—standard gauges are No. 4 ($\frac{1}{8}$-inch diameter) through No. 14 ($\frac{1}{4}$-inch diameter). Sheet-metal screws, with threads extending to the heads, are sized like standard wood screws and are often used to attach plywood panels and hardware.

Bolts.

Though most common in metalwork, bolts, washers, and nuts have important uses in wood construction. Hanger bolts have two types of threads—screw threads at one end and machine threads at the other—and are used to join hardware to wood. Machine and carriage bolts are used to fasten wood in heavy-duty applications; stove bolts join 2-by-4s for lighter structures, such as rough shelving.

Bolts are sized by diameters of the threaded part and by the length from the bottom of the head to the end of the bolt. Flat-head stove bolts, however, are measured from the top of the head.

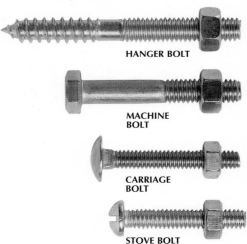

HANGER BOLT

MACHINE BOLT

CARRIAGE BOLT

STOVE BOLT

ANCHORS

Designed to connect framing members together, framing anchors are shaped metal plates fastened by short nails supplied by the manufacturer. Anchors come in many shapes, and are made for a wide range of applications. Originally developed to strengthen joints of buildings in hurricane areas, they are increasingly popular because they eliminate toenailing and difficult hammering angles.

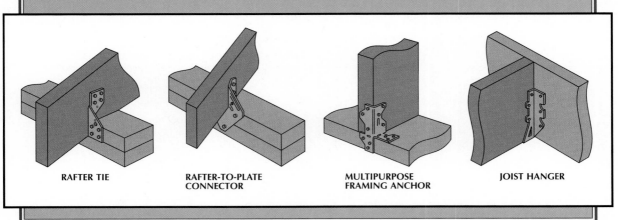

RAFTER TIE

RAFTER-TO-PLATE CONNECTOR

MULTIPURPOSE FRAMING ANCHOR

JOIST HANGER

A FASTENER FOR EVERY JOB

Job	Fastener	Size	Placement	Comments
Baseboard	Finishing nail	$2\frac{1}{2}$"	2 at each corner, 2 at each stud.	Drive 1 nail horizontally through the middle of the board, the other downward at a 45° angle into the sole plate.
Base shoe	Finishing nail	$1\frac{1}{2}$"	16" apart.	Drive nail downward at a 45° angle just above middle of shoe.

Bridging between joists
    Diagonal
    Solid
	
	Box nail
	Box nail
		
		$2\frac{1}{2}$"
		$3\frac{1}{2}$"
			
			2 at each end.
			2 at each end.
				Nail through bridging into joists. Nail through joists into staggered bridging.

Carriage, stair
    To header
    To wall
	
	Common nail
	Common nail
		
		$3\frac{1}{2}$"
		$3\frac{1}{2}$"
			
			6 evenly spaced.
			2 at each stud.
				Use framing anchor where possible.

Casing, door and window	Finishing nail	$1\frac{1}{2}$" 2"	About 12" apart.	Drive $1\frac{1}{2}$" nails on inside edge, 2" nails on outside edge.
Ceiling molding	Finishing nail	$2\frac{1}{2}$"	1 at each corner, 1 at each stud.	

Collar beam to rafter:
    1-by lumber
    2-by lumber
	
	Common nail
	Common nail
		
		$2\frac{1}{2}$"
		$3\frac{1}{4}$
			
			4 at each end.
				Drive 2 nails into beam, 2 into rafter.

Door stop	Finishing nail	$1\frac{1}{2}$"	8" to 10" apart.	
Fascia board	Box nail	2" or $2\frac{1}{2}$"	2 at each rafter.	

Flooring
    " thick
    $\frac{1}{2}$" thick
	
	Spiral or cut nail
	Spiral or cut nail
		
		$2\frac{1}{4}$" or $2\frac{1}{2}$"
		$1\frac{3}{4}$" or 2"
			
			10" to 12" apart.
			8" to 10" apart.
				Angle spiral nails 45° at base of tongue; drive cut nails straight and leave exposed for rustic look.

Header
    Wooden
 	
    Steel-reinforced
	
	Common nail
	
	Carriage bolt
		
		$3\frac{1}{2}$"
		
		$\frac{1}{2}$" x $4\frac{1}{2}$"
			
			Staggered 12" apart.
			
			Staggered 16" apart.
				Drive nails 4" from each end and $\frac{3}{4}$" from each edge.
				Fasten 2 bolts at each end, 4" from edge, 6" from end.

Joist
    Overlap at partition or girder
    To header or band joist
	
	Common nail
		
		$3\frac{1}{2}$"
			
			2 on each side.
				Nail at slight angle.
				
				Use joist hanger.

Job	Fastener	Size	Placement	Comments
Plate				
Partition top plate, across joists	Common nail	3"	2 at each joist.	
Partition top plate, parallel to joists	Common nail	$3\frac{1}{2}$"	24" apart.	Nail to joist or blocking.
Partition sole plate to floor	Common nail	3"	12" apart.	
Bearing wall sole plate, to joist	Common nail	$3\frac{1}{2}$"	16" apart.	
Double top plate	Common nail	$3\frac{1}{2}$"	16" apart.	Lap joints of lower plate 4 feet on both sides.
Rafter				
To ridge beam	Common nail	$3\frac{1}{2}$" and $2\frac{1}{2}$"	3 on each side of beam.	Fasten through edge with $3\frac{1}{2}$" nails, toenail with $2\frac{1}{2}$" nails.
To top plate	Common nail	$2\frac{1}{2}$"	1 on each side.	Toenail or use framing anchor.
Hip or valley rafter, to common rafter	Common nail	3"	2 on one side, 1 on the other.	Toenail.
Jack rafter, to hip rafter	Common nail	3"	2 on one side, 1 on the other.	Toenail.
Riser, stair	Finishing nail	2"	3 at each carriage.	Drill pilot holes in hardwood.
Sheathing				
Roof or wall, $\frac{5}{16}$" or $\frac{3}{8}$" plywood	Common nail	2"	6" apart on edges; 12" apart on intermediate studs or rafters.	
Roof or wall, $\frac{1}{2}$" plywood	Common nail	$2\frac{1}{2}$"	Same as above	
Roof, board	Common nail	$2\frac{1}{2}$"	2 at each rafter.	
Studs				
To top plate	Common nail	$3\frac{1}{2}$"	2 at each end.	
To sole plate	Common nail	$2\frac{1}{2}$"	2 on one side, 1 on the other.	Toenail or use framing anchor.
Cripple studs to headers and sill	Common nail	$3\frac{1}{2}$" or $2\frac{1}{2}$"	2 at ends or 2 on one side, 1 on the other.	Drive $3\frac{1}{2}$" nails through header or sill into studs or toenail $2\frac{1}{2}$" nails.
Jack to king stud	Common nail	$3\frac{1}{2}$"	6 nails evenly spaced and staggered.	Nail at slight angle.
King stud to header	Common nail	$3\frac{1}{2}$"	4 at each end.	
To adjoining wall	Common nail	$3\frac{1}{2}$"	16" apart.	
Subflooring				
$\frac{1}{2}$" plywood	Common nail	2"	6" apart on edges, 10" apart on intermediate joists.	
$\frac{5}{8}$" or $\frac{3}{4}$" plywood	Common nail	$2\frac{1}{2}$"	Same as for $\frac{1}{2}$" plywood.	
Tread, stair	Finishing nail	$2\frac{1}{2}$"	3 at each carriage.	Drill pilot holes in hardwood.
Underlayment to subflooring				
$\frac{3}{8}$" or $\frac{1}{2}$" plywood	Common nail	$1\frac{1}{2}$"	6" apart on edges, 8" apart inside.	
$\frac{3}{8}$" particleboard	Common nail	$1\frac{1}{2}$"	6" apart on edges, 10" apart inside.	

The first hard lesson every amateur carpenter learns is the difficulty of driving a nail straight and true. The skill of the professional comes only with practice, but knowing some basic facts makes expertise easier to acquire.

Choosing the Right Hammer: Good nailing begins with the proper hammer. The ones most used for carpentry come with several types of heads and handles and in several weights. A lightweight 7- or 13-ounce hammer is best for finish work; it drives finishing nails easily and is less likely to mar trim if its face hits the wood. A heavier 16-ounce hammer can be used for finish as well as framing work, and is the preferred weight for general use. The other common size, 20-ounce, is used solely on framing jobs.

Handles are available in wood, steel, and fiberglass. Wooden handles absorb more of the shock of the blows, but they tend to loosen and must be retightened *(below)*. Steel and fiberglass handles rarely come loose, but they vibrate badly when driving large nails; both have padded handles that absorb some of the vibration. Of the two, fiberglass is lighter but more breakable, while steel is virtually indestructible.

Hammer heads are either curved or straight. The curved type works better for pulling nails, while the straight-claw model is used mainly for framing and renovation work; this style of claw more easily wedges between two boards to pry them apart.

Nailing Technique: The correct nailing technique varies not with the type of hammer but with the way the nail is to be driven *(opposite and pages 96-97)*. If you do happen to bend a nail or drive it wrong, do not waste time trying to straighten it. Simply pull it out *(pages 98-99)* and drive a new one.

 TOOLS

Cold chisel
Ball-peen hammer
Hacksaw

Claw hammer
Nail set
Mallet
Cat's paw pry bar
Nail puller

 **MATERIALS**

Hammer-fastening wedge

Common nails
Finishing nails
Scrap wood

SAFETY TIPS

Wear goggles whenever you strike or remove a nail.

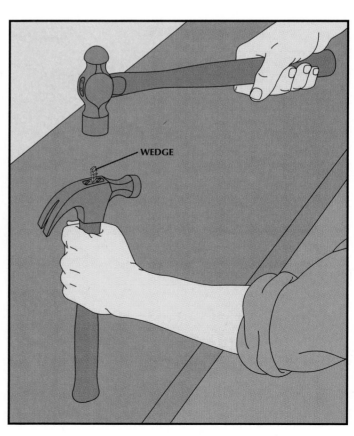

Tightening a wooden handle.

◆ With a cold chisel and a ball-peen hammer, cut a groove $\frac{1}{16}$ inch deep in the top of the handle, halfway between and parallel with the fastening wedges already inserted in the handle top at the factory.

◆ Set a new wedge—sold at hardware stores—into the groove and drive it into the handle with the ball-peen hammer until the wedge barely moves with each blow *(right)*. (If you drive it further, you may split the handle.)

◆ With a hacksaw, cut off all the protruding portion of the wedge flush with the top of the hammerhead.

WEDGE

TECHNIQUES FOR DRIVING NAILS

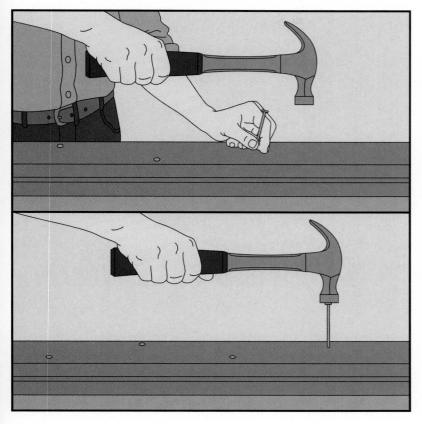

Starting and driving a nail.
◆ Hold the nail near its tip between your thumb and index finger, angle it about 10 degrees away from you, and tap it lightly with a claw hammer *(left, top)*—the nail will straighten under the hammer blows. Support the nail with your fingers until it is driven deep enough into the wood to stand by itself.
◆ Swing the hammer up to a point just behind your ear; then, deliver the blow so that, when the hammer strikes the nail, the handle is at a 90-degree angle with the nail shaft, and the nailhead is directly below the center of its face *(left, bottom)*.
◆ For the last blow, adjust the force of the hammer to drive the head of the nail flush with the wood surface.

Nailing out.
When you must drive a nail located between knee and shoulder height in a space too restricted for a normal swing, nail horizontally in front of your body with a stroke called nailing out: Grip the hammer with your thumb on the back of the handle for better control. Holding the hammer with its head in front of you, bend your arm back toward your body, and drive the nail by swinging your arm outward *(right)*.

Nailing up.

When the nail you are driving is above your head, grip the hammer as you would for nailing out *(page 95)* and swing your arm upward with a full wrist, elbow, and shoulder motion. If the work is so high that your arm would be almost fully extended at the end of the swing and the hammer cannot hit the nail squarely, stand on a ladder to provide a better striking position *(right)*.

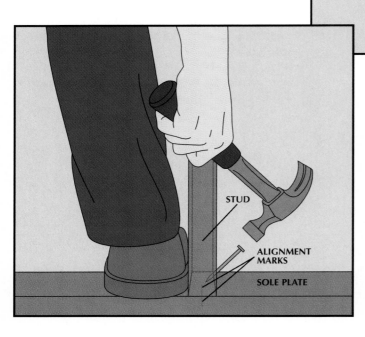

STUD

ALIGNMENT MARKS

SOLE PLATE

Toenailing.

In some situations, you will have to drive nails at a slant to penetrate two pieces of wood—a technique called toenailing.

◆ To help align the toenailed board with the piece it will be nailed into (in this case, a stud being fastened to a sole plate), hold the pieces in position and draw a short straight line along the middle of the stud and onto the sole plate.

◆ Brace the stud with your toes or the side of your foot and drive the first nail at an angle until its point just exits the bottom of the stock.

◆ Line up the two pencil lines and strike the nail sharply to lock the stud in place *(left)*. Then drive the nail home.

◆ Toenail the pieces together on the other side. Check the pencil lines; if the two parts have been displaced, hammer one side of the toenailed piece to bring the lines together.

THE PRO'S CHOICE FOR QUICK NAILING: AN AIR-POWERED NAIL GUN

If you will be doing a lot of nailing—laying decking, reroofing with asphalt shingles, or installing a houseful of molding, for example—consider buying or renting an air-powered nailer. Hooked up to a compressor, the model shown at right can drive nails ranging from 2 to $3\frac{1}{2}$ inches with the touch of a trigger, but there are also models suitable for finish carpentry. All of them feature a safety device to prevent the accidental firing of a nail.

Clinch-nailing.

Clinch-nailing is the technique to use when you need to join two boards together face-to-face, such as for a composite header or a support board. Choose nails that are 30 percent longer than the combined thickness of the two boards.

◆ Drive the nailheads flush, then turn the pieces over and set them on a hard, flat surface. Hammer the projecting nail shanks at an angle, bending them as close to the surface as possible *(right)*. Align the shanks with the grain for a smoother surface, but across the grain for a stronger joint.

◆ When the shanks are nearly horizontal, strike them with two or three blows to seat them deeply in the wood.

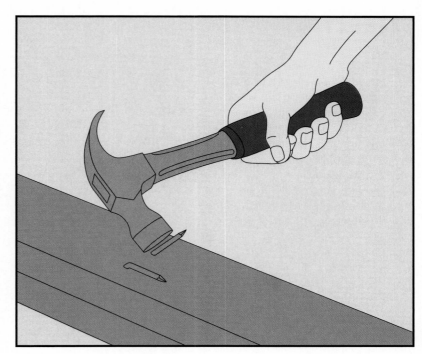

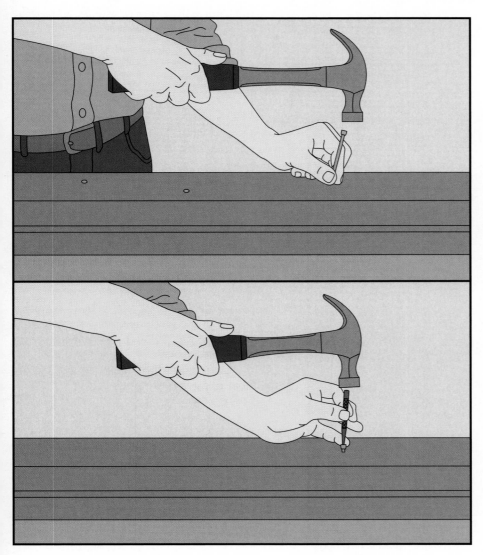

Driving and setting a finishing nail.

◆ Hold the nail as you would for rough work *(page 95)*, but wrap your fingers around the hammer handle and set your thumb along the handle as shown *(left, top)*. Hit the nail lightly, supporting it with your fingers until it can stand by itself, then drive it until its head is about $\frac{1}{8}$ inch above the surface of the wood.

◆ Hold a nail set between thumb and index finger and center the tip over the head of the nail. Rest your little finger on the wood to steady your hand, then hit the top of the nail set solidly with the hammer to drive the head of the nail about $\frac{1}{16}$ inch below the surface of the wood *(left, bottom)*.

EXTRACTING NAILS

Starting an embedded nail.
◆ Using a curved-claw hammer, set the end of the claw on the wood just next to the nailhead and strike the face of the hammer with a mallet until the claw engages the nailhead *(right)*.
◆ Pull the handle of the hammer to a nearly vertical position and disengage the claw from the nailhead.
◆ Remove the partially raised nail as described below.

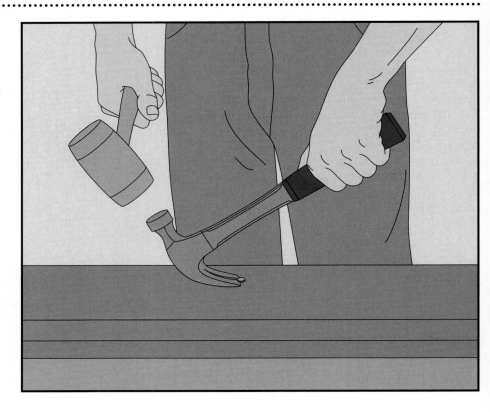

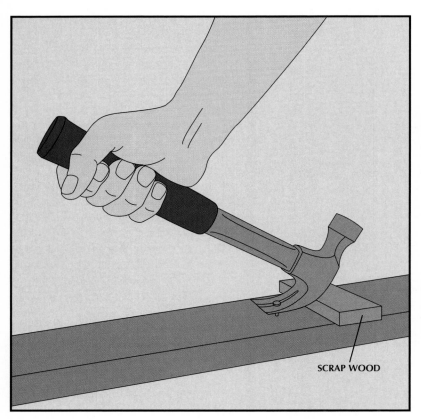

SCRAP WOOD

Removing a partially raised nail.
◆ If the nailhead is just above the surface, slide the claw of a curved-claw hammer underneath it and pivot the hammer's handle up to raise the nail slightly.
◆ Place a piece of scrap wood—about as thick as the height of the half-pulled nail above the surface—next to the nail and set the head of the hammer on the scrap.
◆ Slip the claw around the nailhead and pull the nail out of the board *(left)*.

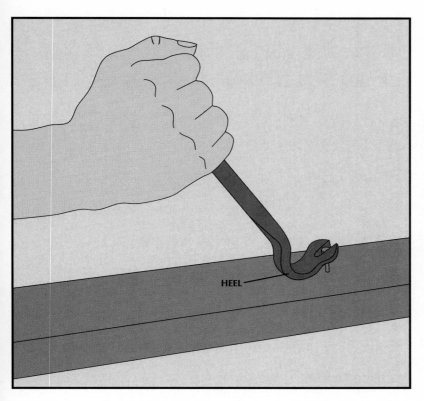

Pulling nails with a pry bar.

◆ Set the claw of a cat's paw pry bar around the head of the nail; if the head is below the surface of the wood, strike the curved section at the back of the tool with a mallet to drive the claw under the head. If you are pulling a nail from finish trim, set a thin piece of scrap wood under the heel of the cat's paw to protect the wood.

◆ Pull back on the handle to remove the nail *(left)*.

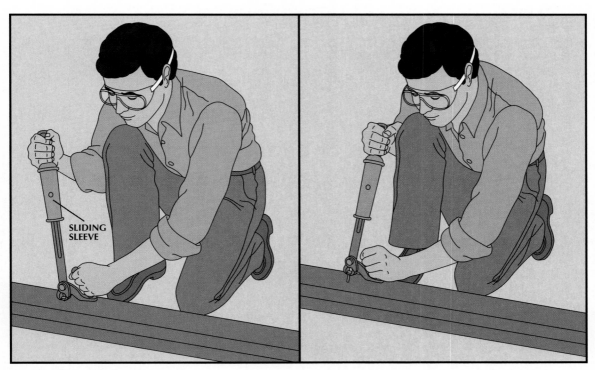

Removing a stubborn nail.

◆ Position the pincers of a nail puller above the nailhead, opening them so they are slightly wider than the nailhead *(above, left)*.

◆ Hold the handle attached to the pincers, then raise the sliding metal sleeve and slam it down repeatedly to sink the pincers beneath the nailhead.

◆ Close the pincers around the head.

◆ Tilt the pincers sideways *(above, right)*, using the short handle attached to the pincers as a lever, and slowly remove the nail.

Screws have several advantages over nails as fasteners of wood. They bind pieces tighter, they do not mar the surface either entering or exiting, and with the proper pilot holes they do not split wood. But since they take more time to install than nails and are more expensive, they are reserved for joints that need extra strength or precision assembly—or that may have to be dismantled.

Preparing Screw Holes: All screws need at least one hole and some call for as many as four. A pilot hole is required for screws that are threaded all the way to the head, like sheet-metal screws or the screws often supplied with hardware kits or used for plywood. The hole is drilled with a bit slightly smaller than the diameter of the screw threads.

Other screws require additional holes: Standard wood screws and lag screws have smooth shanks between their threads and their heads; to accommodate the shank, a clearance hole—a shallow hole slightly larger than the pilot hole—is needed. If the screwhead is to be set flush with or below the surface of the wood—a necessity with flat-head screws but optional with other types—a very shallow countersink hole the diameter of the screwhead is needed. Finally, to hide a screwhead, a straight-sided counterbore hole can be drilled to accommodate a wood plug on top of the screw. While a tiered screw hole can be made with regular bits used one after the other, a special bit does the entire job in a single step *(opposite, top)*.

Choosing a Screwdriver. A screwdriver must have the appropriate style and size of tip for the screw slot—straight, Phillips, or square-drive, as shown on page 91. There are screwdrivers for special needs, with offset right-angle handles, extra-short or long shanks, or easy-to-grip knob handles. For driving screws quickly, some carpenters rely on a spiral-ratchet screwdriver. An electric drill—consider a cordless model for convenience—can be fitted with a screwdriver bit, providing quicker results *(opposite, bottom)*, but use it only when marring the wood is of no consequence—the bit can chew into the wood if it slips from the screwhead.

TOOLS

Electric drill
Combination countersink-counterbore bit
Screwdriver bit

SAFETY TIPS

Put on goggles when operating a power tool.

TRICKS OF THE TRADE

Shop-Made Depth Guide

Drilling a pilot hole to a precise depth is easy with the help of a jig like the one shown at right. With the bit installed in the drill's chuck, subtract the desired drilling depth from the length of bit protruding from the chuck. Cut a piece of 1-by-1 stock to this length, then bore a hole through its center. Drill the pilot hole, stopping when the guide touches the workpiece.

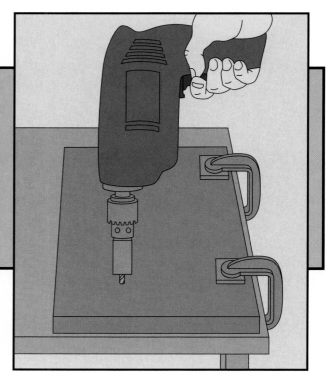

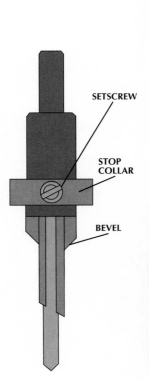

SETSCREW

STOP
COLLAR

BEVEL

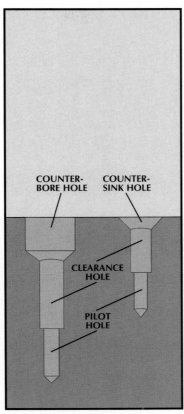

COUNTER-
BORE HOLE

COUNTER-
SINK HOLE

CLEARANCE
HOLE

PILOT
HOLE

A combination bit to recess screws.

◆ Select the correct size of combination countersink-counterbore bit for the screw to be driven.

◆ Position the stop collar at the appropriate position on the shank: For a counterbore hole, the collar is set the same distance above the top of the beveled part as the desired depth of the hole, like the bit at left. For a countersink hole, the collar is set over the beveled part of the shank.

◆ Tighten the setscrew to lock the collar in place, then install the bit in an electric drill and bore the hole *(page 46)*.

Driving screws with a drill.

Phillips-head screws are best suited to drills—the bit tends to slip out of the straight-slot type more easily.

◆ With one hand gripping the drill handle, set the palm of the other on top of the motor housing for working vertically—or underneath the motor housing for working horizontally—and drive the screw at low speed *(right)*.

◆ Stop drilling when the screw is in place—additional revolutions will strip the threads carved in the wood or break off the screwhead.

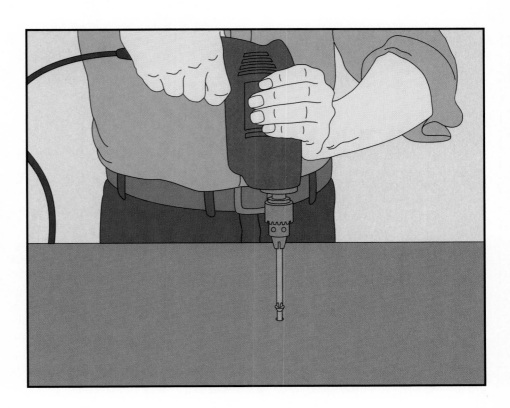

Joining Wood with Biscuits

Plate joiners, also known as biscuit joiners, are ideally suited for building carcasses—the boxes that serve as the base for many furniture projects. The tool features a retractable, spring-mounted blade that cuts slots in mating pieces. Glue is applied in the slots and an oval-shaped "biscuit" of compressed beech is inserted. Made in various sizes depending on the thickness of the stock to be joined, the wafers rapidly absorb the glue and swell, making a very solid joint.

Preparing for the Job: A typical cabinet is made from $\frac{3}{4}$-inch-thick stock *(below)*. Cut the sides, top, and bottom to size so the grain of all the pieces will run in the same direction when the cabinet is assembled. For $\frac{3}{4}$-inch-thick boards, adjust the joiner to cut slots for No. 10 biscuits.

 TOOLS

Plate joiner
C-clamps
Bar clamps

 **MATERIALS**

Support board
Biscuits
Wood glue

 SAFETY TIPS

Put on goggles when cutting slots for biscuits with a plate joiner.

Anatomy of a plate joiner.
To cut a slot with the joiner, the housing is pushed forward so the blade protrudes through its opening and plunges into the stock. When not in operation, the blade is hidden inside the body. A guideline on the faceplate helps you align the blade with the work. Available in three standard sizes, the wood biscuits range in length from $1\frac{13}{16}$ to $2\frac{3}{16}$ inches *(photograph)*. No. 0, the shortest, is for wood $\frac{1}{4}$ to $\frac{1}{2}$ inch thick. Use No. 10 for $\frac{1}{2}$- to $\frac{3}{4}$-inch-thick wood, and No. 20 for thicker boards.

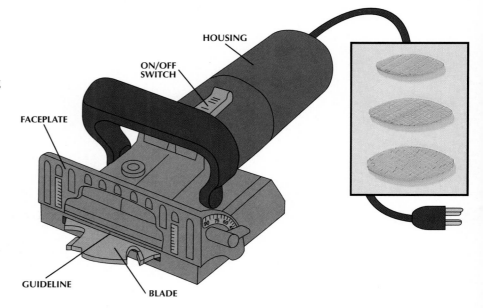

CONSTRUCTING A CARCASS

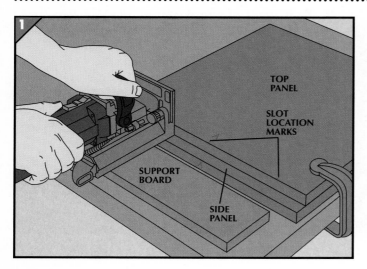

1. Cutting slots in the top panel.
◆ Lay one of the side panels outside-face down on a work surface and set the top piece outside-face up on top of it, adding reference letters to identify adjacent edges.
◆ Set the edge of the top panel back by an amount equal to the thickness of the stock, then clamp the two pieces in place.
◆ Place a support board the same thickness as the stock in front of the workpieces, then mark slot location lines on the top panel every 6 inches.
◆ Resting the plate joiner on the support board, align the guideline on the faceplate with a slot location mark on the stock. Holding the tool with both hands, push in the housing to make the cut *(left)*. Repeat the process at the other marks.

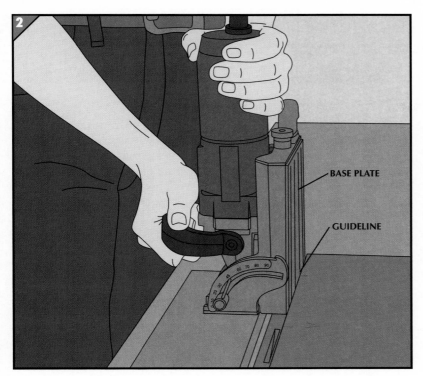

2. Slotting the side panels.

◆ Holding the plate joiner upright, align the guideline in the center of the tool's base plate with a slot mark and make a cut.

◆ Cut the rest of the grooves along the edge *(left)*, then repeat the clamping and cutting procedure on the opposite edge, and then on the bottom panel and other side panel.

BASE PLATE

GUIDELINE

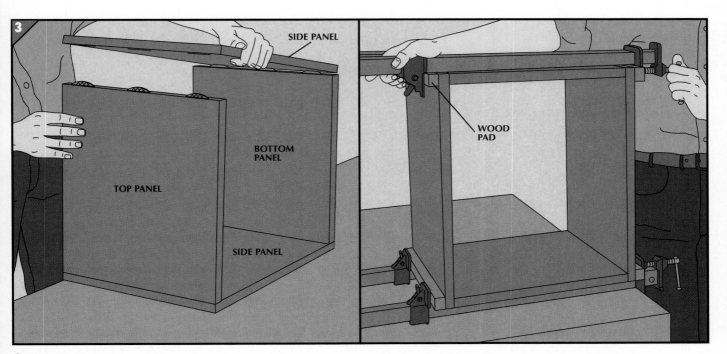

SIDE PANEL

TOP PANEL

BOTTOM PANEL

SIDE PANEL

WOOD PAD

3. Gluing up the carcass.

◆ Set the side panels face down on the work surface.

◆ Squeeze a bead of wood glue into the slots and along the edges of the top and bottom panels, then spread it evenly over the surface of the edges.

◆ Insert the biscuits in their slots, then assemble the carcass, fitting the top and bottom panels down onto one side and then adding the other side *(above, left)*.

◆ Install two bar clamps across the top and bottom, protecting the workpieces with wood pads.

◆ Tighten the clamps a little at a time until the glue starts to squeeze out of the joints *(above, right)*.

◆ Check the carcass for square by measuring the diagonals between opposite corners. If they are not equal, install a fifth clamp across the longer diagonal and tighten it until the carcass is square.

Trim Joints: Tests of Craftsmanship

Trim carpentry—the craft of making neat, tightly jointed frames around doors, windows, and walls—is one of the most demanding tests of woodworking skill. It requires not only mastery of the basic techniques of cutting and shaping wood, but also a repertoire of tricks for fitting and fastening the pieces.

Miter Joints: The simplest, most common joint is the miter, which takes molding around a corner *(below and pages 105-106)*. On door and window casing, the face of the molding is cut at an angle for the miter. On inside corner joints (between baseboards that meet at the corner of a room, for example), the end of one piece may need to be cut to follow the molded curve of another—a technique called coping *(page 107)*.

Marking, Cutting, and Nailing: Precise marking is essential for professional results. With casing and interior corners, always nail one piece before you mark the next, so that you will have a benchmark to measure from. Cut moldings a fraction of an inch longer—$\frac{1}{16}$ inch for a short piece of casing, as much as $\frac{1}{4}$ inch for a long baseboard—since there is no good remedy for a piece that is too short. If you plan to apply a clear finish to the trim, it will be difficult to conceal gaps. Take extra care to cut precise joints.

Trim is easily split by nails. Blunt the points with a hammer or drill pilot holes.

 TOOLS

Combination square
Miter box with
  backsaw
Hammer
Tape measure
Dovetail saw
Nail set
Putty knife
Coping saw
Utility knife
Block plane

 **MATERIALS**

Casing stock
Finishing nails
Wood putty or
  spackling compound
Baseboard molding
Cornice molding
Shoe molding
Window trim
Wood glue
Masking tape

 SAFETY TIPS

Wear goggles when nailing.

DOOR AND WINDOW CASING

1. Nailing the top casing.

◆ On doors and casement windows, measure from the inside edge of the jambs to set the casing $\frac{1}{8}$ inch above the inner edge of the window or door jamb; in doing so, you will avoid having to cut mortises for the hinges. (On double-hung windows, you can set the casing flush with the inside of the jambs.)
◆ Cut the ends of the top casing at a 45-degree angle *(page 30)* and hold the casing in place over the head jamb.
◆ Drive a finishing nail partway through the casing into the jamb at each corner, then nail the upper edge of the casing to the header over the jamb at 12-inch intervals *(left)*, leaving about $\frac{1}{8}$ inch of the nails protruding.
◆ Nail the lower edge of the casing to the jamb, placing the nails directly below those in the upper edge.

2. Fitting the side casing.

◆ Mark the thin edge of the stock for the side casing $\frac{1}{16}$ inch longer than is necessary for an exact fit—extending from the bottom of the top casing miter to the stool of a window or, for a door, to the floor *(right)*.

◆ Square off the bottom of the stock and miter the top end, making the thick edge longer than the thin one.

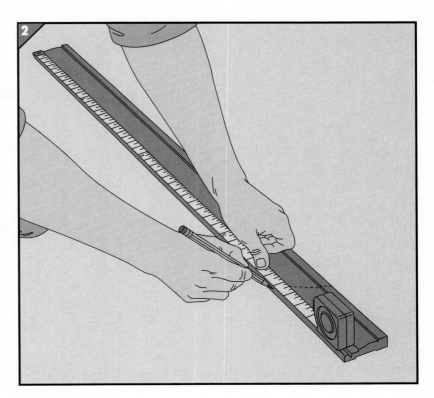

3. Nailing on the side casing.

Fit the side casing as tight as possible against the top casing and, at 12-inch intervals, drive finishing nails partway—leaving about $\frac{1}{4}$ inch protruding—through the side casing into the side jamb *(left)*, then drive nails into the stud.

SIDE JAMB

4. Adjusting the casing.

If you find gaps, first try to close them by tapping against the sides with a hammer and wood block. If the joint remains ragged with edges meeting at only a few points, tape a piece of cardboard to the wall as protection, then cut along the joint line with a small backsaw called a dovetail saw *(right)*, then tap the casing again.

5. Lock-nailing the joint.

◆ To keep the joint firmly fastened and prevent it from opening when the wood shrinks, hold the side casing firmly in place and drive a finishing nail long enough to penetrate through the top casing into the side casing *(left)*.

◆ Drive a second nail horizontally through the side casing into the top casing.

◆ Countersink all the nails with a nail set.

◆ With a putty knife, fill the holes with wood putty if you plan to stain the casing; otherwise apply spackling compound.

COPING A JOINT

1. Marking the molding.

◆ Butt the square end of a piece of molding into the corner and nail the molding to the wall.

◆ Miter the end of a second piece at 45 degrees, angling the cut so that the back side of the molding will be longer than the front face.

◆ Mark along the curved profile line with the side of a pencil to make the profile more visible *(right)*.

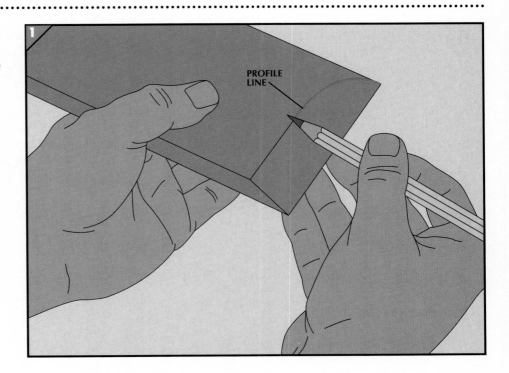

PROFILE LINE

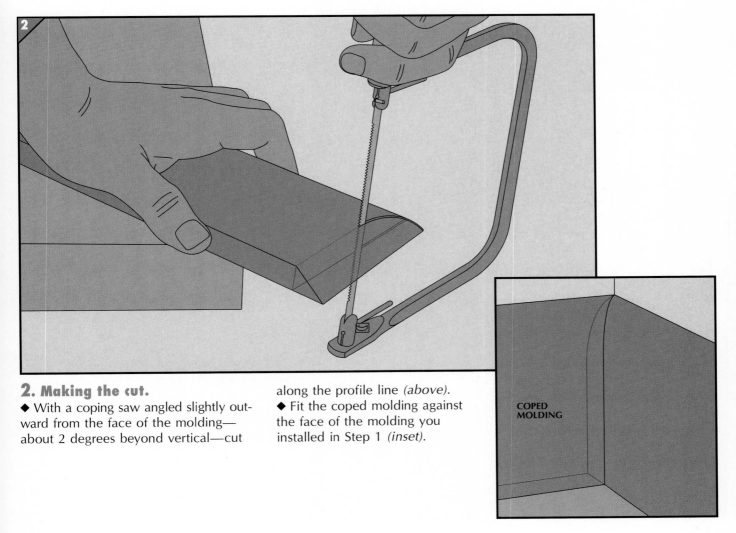

2. Making the cut.

◆ With a coping saw angled slightly outward from the face of the molding—about 2 degrees beyond vertical—cut along the profile line *(above)*.

◆ Fit the coped molding against the face of the molding you installed in Step 1 *(inset)*.

COPED MOLDING

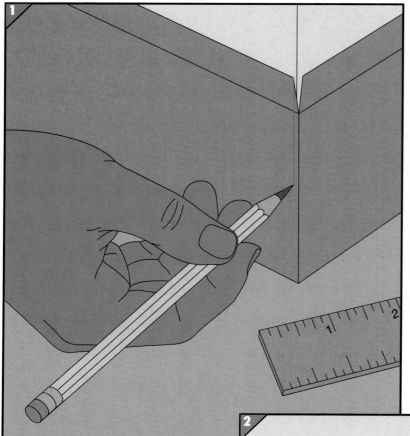

1. Measuring the gap.

When you have cut a 45-degree miter and the corner angle is greater than 90 degrees, the molding will open at the back. You can correct the problem by fine-tuning the joint.

◆ Hold the moldings in place and measure the gap between the two pieces.

◆ If the gap is less than $\frac{1}{4}$ inch, mark a line on one piece of molding at the measured distance from the corner *(left)*. If the gap is more than $\frac{1}{4}$ inch, mark half the measurement on each piece of molding.

2. Planing to correct the fit.

◆ Secure the piece of molding in a vise.

◆ With a block plane, carefully plane the molding down to the marked line, working from each edge toward the middle to avoid tearout and angling the tool to correspond to the marked line in the illustration at right.

◆ If you marked both pieces in Step 1, repeat the process on the second one.

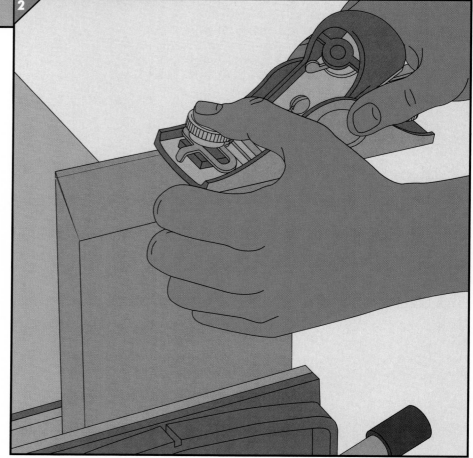

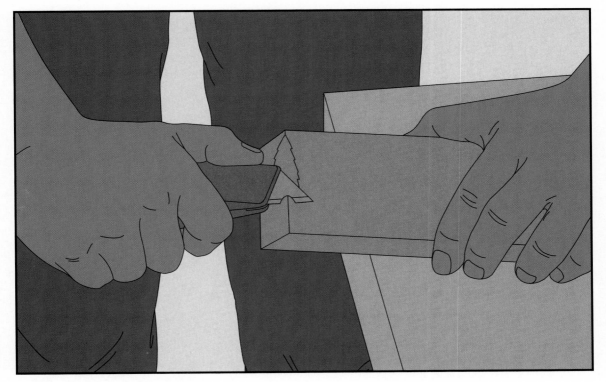

Shaving with a utility knife.

If the wall angle is less than 90 degrees, molding with standard 45-degree miters will open at the front. Fixing the problem depends on the size of the gap and the width of the molding. For a gap less than $\frac{1}{4}$ inch on molding up to 4 inches wide, shave slivers of wood from the inner edge of one piece of molding with a utility knife (*above*); for larger molding, make the cuts with a coping saw. To correct a large gap, shave wood from both sides of the joint. Start just below the top of the molding—do not shave the top, which will squeeze to a tight fit—and work down to the bottom of the joint.

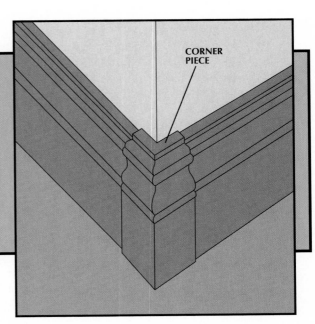

TRICKS OF THE TRADE

Time-Saving Corner Pieces

In many cases, you can buy ready-made corner pieces to match the molding (*right*), which will save you the trouble of mitering. Nail the corner molding in place and butt the adjoining sections against it. If the corner is not square, mark the gap between corner piece and the adjoining sections (*opposite, Step 1*), then plane the corner piece to fit flush against both ends.

CORNER PIECE

MATCHING THE ANGLES OF A STAIRCASE

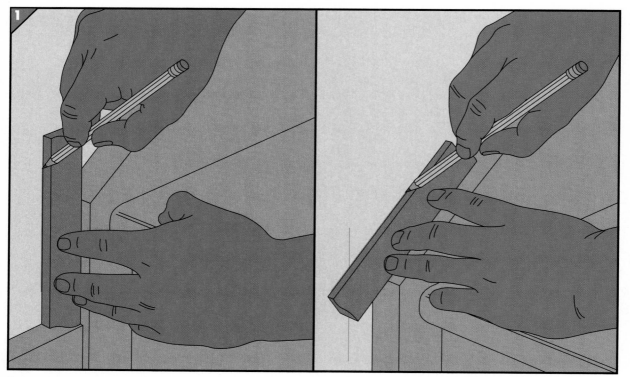

1. Marking the wall.
◆ Place the bottom of a piece of molding along one side of the angle and use the top as a straightedge while marking a line on the wall *(above, left)*.
◆ Move the molding to the other side of the angle and draw a second line on the wall that intersects the first *(above, right)*.

2. Marking and cutting the molding.
◆ Hold a piece of molding in position along the first side of the angle; mark the top edge of the molding at the intersection of the marked lines on the wall, and the bottom edge at the apex of the angle *(right)*.
◆ Repeat the procedure with a second piece of molding held along the top side of the angle.
◆ Join the marks on each piece of molding, forming cutting lines, and make the cut with a backsaw and miter box.

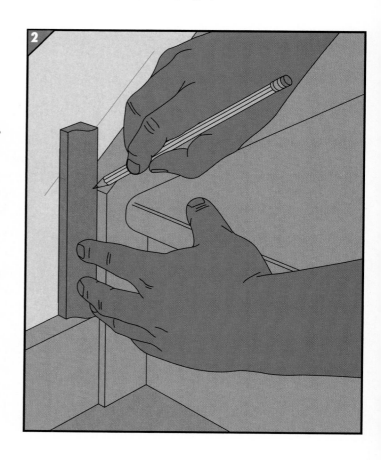

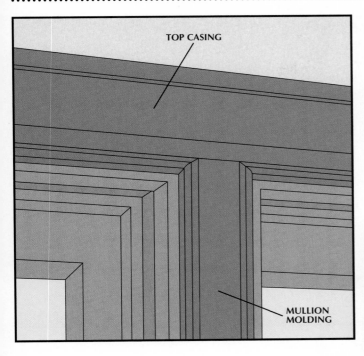

TOP CASING

MULLION MOLDING

Molding for a sectional window or door.

To trim a window containing two or more sections, or to trim a transom over a door, you need special casing stock called mullion or transom molding. For a multisection window, the mullion is placed between the sections and fits into a notch cut into the top casing *(left)*. On a door with a transom, the molding runs horizontally between the door and transom, and fits into notches in the side casings.

1. Mitering the mullion molding.

◆ To shape the molding to fit into the top casing, mark cut lines at 45-degree angles on the beads on each side of the molding.
◆ Place the molding in a miter box, adjust the saw to the angle, and make the cut *(right)*.

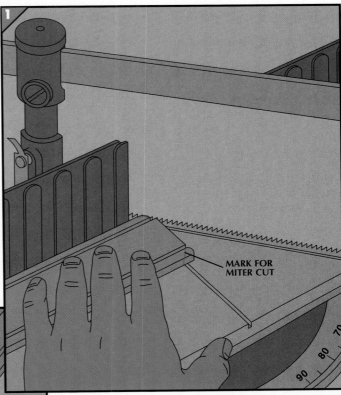

MARK FOR MITER CUT

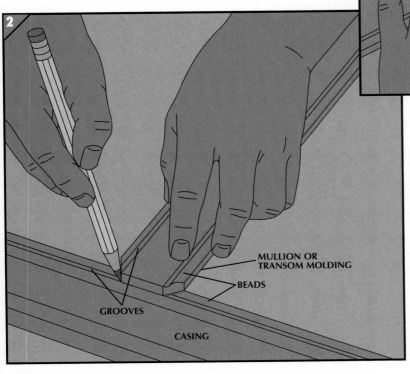

GROOVES

MULLION OR TRANSOM MOLDING

BEADS

CASING

2. Notching the casing.

◆ Place the mitered end of the molding over the bead of the casing and draw lines on the casing along each miter cut *(left)*.
◆ With a coping saw, cut out the section of casing between the lines so the end of the molding will fit tightly into the body of the casing, with the beads of the molding and casing forming neat miter joints.
◆ Miter the other end in the same way for a transom; for a mullion, cut the bottom end square so it butts against the stool.

SPLICING MOLDING ALONG A WALL

Making a scarf joint.
If the wall is longer than the molding, you can splice two pieces to fit; be sure to make the joint at a stud.
◆ Miter the ends of the two pieces at 45 degrees in the same direction by setting the miter-box saw in the same position for both pieces.
◆ Drive finishing nails through the splice long enough to penetrate the stud by $\frac{1}{2}$ inch *(right)*.

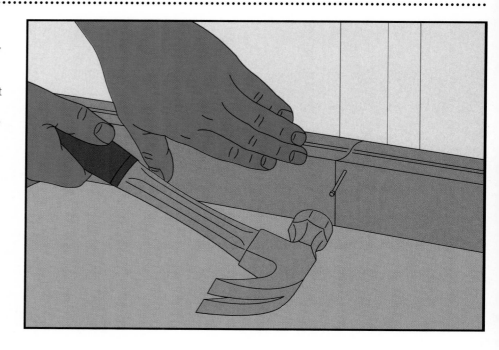

COVERING AN EXPOSED END

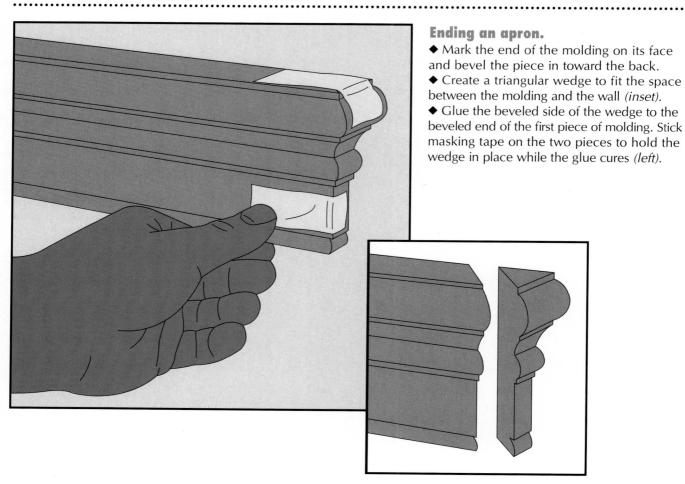

Ending an apron.
◆ Mark the end of the molding on its face and bevel the piece in toward the back.
◆ Create a triangular wedge to fit the space between the molding and the wall *(inset)*.
◆ Glue the beveled side of the wedge to the beveled end of the first piece of molding. Stick masking tape on the two pieces to hold the wedge in place while the glue cures *(left)*.

Ending a window stool.
◆ Miter the end of the window stool.
◆ Cut a scrap of trim into a triangular wedge to fit the mitered end of the stool, with a square cut at the other end.
◆ Glue the end piece in place *(right)*, then secure it to the stool with finishing nails.

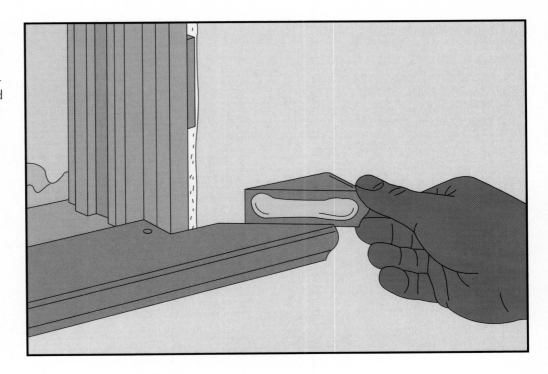

A PLINTH FOR AN AWKWARD CORNER

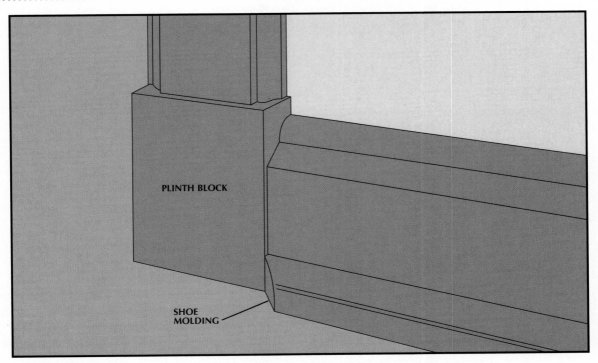

PLINTH BLOCK

SHOE
MOLDING

A plinth block.
◆ Where different moldings meet at floor level—in this typical example, a traditional door molding and a more stylized baseboard—cut a rectangular "plinth" block of scrap wood, making it slightly wider, higher, and thicker than each of the moldings.
◆ If the plinth block is more than 3 inches wide, nail it in place; for smaller pieces, glue them to the wall and to the ends of the moldings.
◆ Miter the shoe molding so its end meets the outer edge of the block *(above)*.

MITERING A CEILING MOLDING

An inside corner.

◆ To join two pieces of crown molding at an inside corner *(inset)*, measure the wall from corner to corner, mark the distance on the bottom edge of a length of molding, and place the molding upside down in a miter box.

◆ Cut the molding at a 45-degree angle, holding the bottom of the piece tightly against the fence.

◆ Place the mating piece on the opposite side of the saw blade from its position on the ceiling—to the right side of the blade for the left-hand corner piece and vice versa.

◆ Set the saw for a 45-degree cut to the right to cut the left-hand piece *(right)*; for a right-hand piece, set the handle to the left. Then make the cut.

For a neater but somewhat more difficult alternative, adapt the technique on page 107 and cope the corner joint.

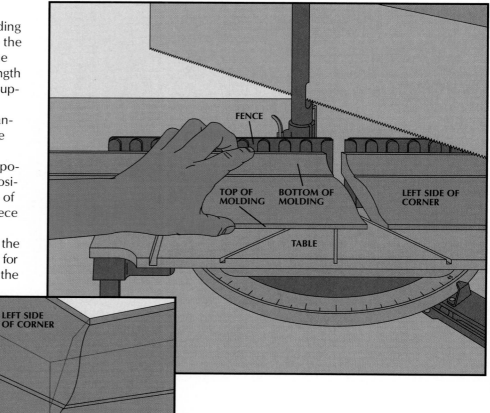

FENCE

TOP OF MOLDING

BOTTOM OF MOLDING

LEFT SIDE OF CORNER

TABLE

LEFT SIDE OF CORNER

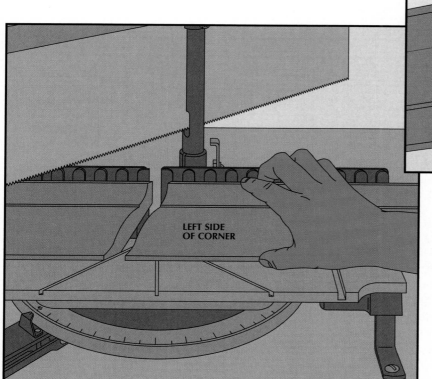

LEFT SIDE OF CORNER

LEFT SIDE OF CORNER

An outside corner.

For an outside corner *(inset)*, place the ceiling molding upside down in the miter box. Rest the flat surfaces of each end against the side and bottom of the miter box as if the side of the box were the wall and the bottom of the box were the ceiling. Cut the piece for the left side of the corner with the saw handle at the left *(left)*, and the piece for the right side with the handle at the right. If the pieces do not fit exactly, pare down the back or front of the miters.

Although houses are no longer held together by strong, interlocking wooden joints, traditional woodworking joints are still needed for many special parts of a modern home—for floors, stairways, and door and window frames.

Dadoes and Rabbets: Technically, a dado is a channel that runs across the grain, and a groove is cut with the grain, but the term dado is frequently used to describe both. The stronger is the dado joint *(below)*, in which the square end of one board fits into a channel near the end of

the other. In the slightly weaker rabbet joint *(page 116)*, a square end fits into a matching step at the end of the other board. Dado joints are used in house framing and on stair treads and risers. Window and door frames often rely on rabbet joints.

For boards that meet edge to edge on a flat surface, such as interior wall paneling, the joint must combine a neat appearance with flexibility so the wood can expand and contract slightly as moisture changes. On interior paneling and exterior siding, boards are often milled with a rabbet along the face

of one edge and a matching rabbet along the back of the other *(pages 117 and 119)*. Paneling and siding also can be fitted together with tongue-and-groove joints *(pages 117 and 120)*: Each board has a groove milled along the center of one edge and a matching tongue on the other.

Mortise-and-Tenon Joints: In this joint, the projecting tenon at the end of one board fits into a socket or hole in the edge of the other. The mortise-and-tenon joint *(pages 121-125)* is commonly used in window sashes and paneled doors.

 TOOLS

Hammer
Nail set
Block plane
Carpenter's level
Mallet

Circular saw
Mortise gauge
Mortise chisel
Lock mortise chisel
Bevel-edge chisel
Skew chisel
Combination square

Utility knife
C-clamp
Backsaw
Pipe clamps
Carpenter's square

 MATERIALS

Lumber
2 x 4s
Plywood ($\frac{1}{4}$")
Finishing nails ($1\frac{1}{2}$")
Wood glue

 **SAFETY TIPS**

Wear safety goggles when hammering.

RIGHT-ANGLE JOINTS WITH DADOES AND RABBETS

A dado joint.

Under the eave of a house roof *(right)*, the edge of the plywood soffit fits into a dado cut in the back of the fascia board, forming a strong, weathertight joint. The dado—its depth ordinarily one-third to one-half the thickness of the fascia board—prevents the soffit from moving up or down; the joint can work loose only if the soffit and fascia board pull apart.

Dado joints also fit the top edge of stair risers to the underside of treads. The same joint can be used between the ends of boards: The top and bottom jambs of a window and the top jamb of a door frame often fit into dadoes in the side jambs.

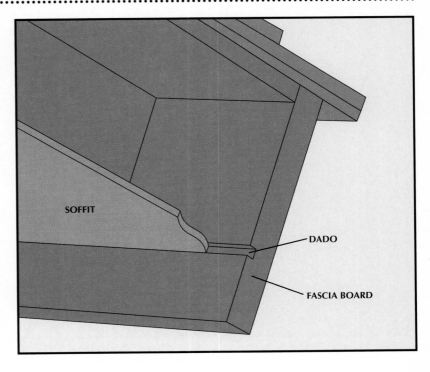

SOFFIT

DADO

FASCIA BOARD

A rabbet joint.

At the bottom of a window frame *(right)*, the sill fits into a step, or rabbet, in the side jamb. Rabbet joints are sometimes used at the tops of door and window frames, where the ends of the top jamb meet the side jambs. The same joint can be used between the edges of boards: The back edge of a stairway tread may fit into a rabbet at the bottom of the riser above it, for example.

Rabbet joints are somewhat weaker than dado joints; however, because a rabbet joint forms a square corner, it can fit into a stair carriage or a door frame, while a dado joint cannot.

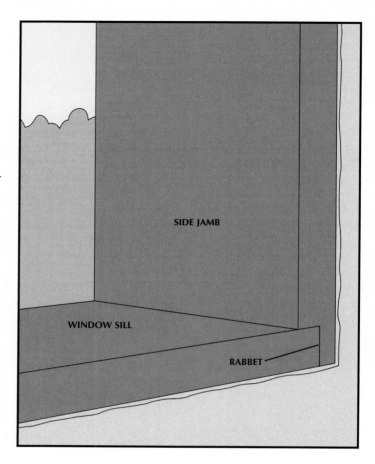

SIDE JAMB

WINDOW SILL

RABBET

TREAD

DADO

RABBET

RISER

A rabbet-and-dado joint.

On a staircase *(left)*, the back of each tread is rabbeted to fit into a dado near the bottom of each riser. The resulting rabbet-and-dado joint combines the best of both types: It is nearly as strong as a dado, but can be made at the edge of a board like a rabbet. In such a stairway, the tops of the risers and the fronts of the treads often are joined in the same way, but as a matter of convenience only; a simple dado would work just as well there.

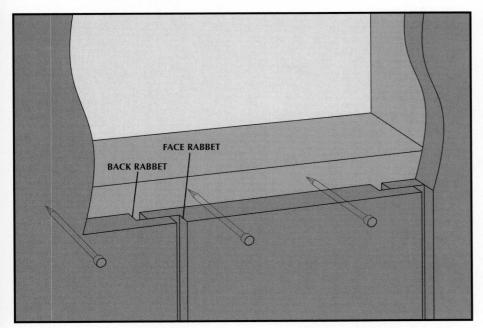

Shiplap joints.
In interior-wall paneling like the type shown at left, each board has a rabbet cut along one edge of the exposed face and another along the opposite edge at the back—a configuration often referred to as a shiplap joint. The projection at the face overlaps the back rabbet to conceal gaps. The space—called a reveal—between each projection and the body of the next board allows boards to expand and contract without buckling or splitting as humidity levels fluctuate. The shiplap joint can also be used for horizontal paneling or, without the gaps between boards, for weathertight exterior siding.

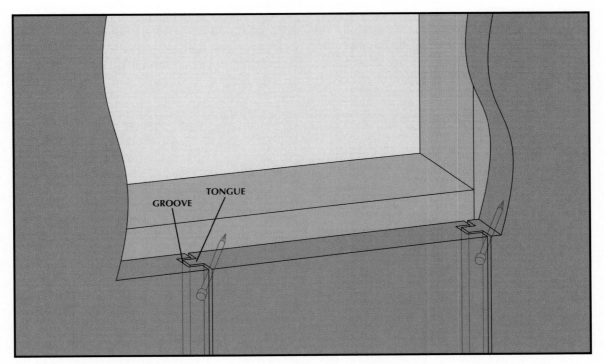

Tongue-and-groove joints.
In the paneling shown above, each board has a groove milled along the center of one edge and a matching tongue along the other. The tongues and grooves interlock in nearly invisible joints and the boards are fastened with "blind nails" driven at an angle through the tongue of each board so they are hidden by the groove of the next board. Stronger than rabbet joints, tongue-and-groove joints are used for wood flooring because they resist squeaking and warping; for plywood subflooring because they eliminate the need for rows of blocking to support the edges of the sheets; and for exterior siding because they resist air infiltration.

A dado joint.

◆ Fit the end of one board into the dado in a second board.

◆ Drive pairs of finishing nails in V patterns *(inset)* through the dado, from the second board into the first *(above)*. The opposing angles of the nails will help keep the joint tight. If the first board is thicker than than $\frac{1}{2}$ inch and too warped to slip easily into the dado, plane the end of the board down; forcing such a board into place could cause it to split.

A rabbet joint.

◆ Fit the end of one board into a rabbet in a second board. Then drive a pair of finishing nails in a V pattern through the rabbet into the end of the unrabbeted board, angling the nails toward the middle of the board, and bracing the other end against a wall to keep the joint tight while you nail.

◆ Drive a second pair of nails through the unrabbeted board into the end of the rabbeted one *(above)*, starting the nails near the middle of the board and angling them toward the edges.

INSTALLING RABBETED PANELS

1. Aligning the first boards.

◆ Between each pair of studs, nail three 2-by-4 nailing blocks, one near the top plate, one near the sole plate, and one at the middle.

◆ If you are paneling only one wall, begin by fitting the square edge of a board against the corner. If you are paneling both walls that meet at a corner, you need a rabbet along both edges of the first board—a 1-inch rabbet on the outside edge; and on the corner edge, a rabbet equal to the board thickness plus the width of the planned gap between boards. With $1\frac{1}{2}$-inch finishing nails, fasten the first board to the top and sole plates and to the blocks, keeping the board plumb with a carpenter's level; drive two nails through the board face—but not the rabbet—at each point.

◆ Set a $\frac{1}{4}$-inch plywood spacer into the rabbet of the first board near the top of the wall, slide the edge of the next board against the spacer, and nail the board to the top plate.

◆ Place the spacer in the rabbet near the bottom of the board and nail the board to the bottom plate; then nail the board to the nailing blocks.

◆ Repeat this procedure for each of the succeeding four boards (right).

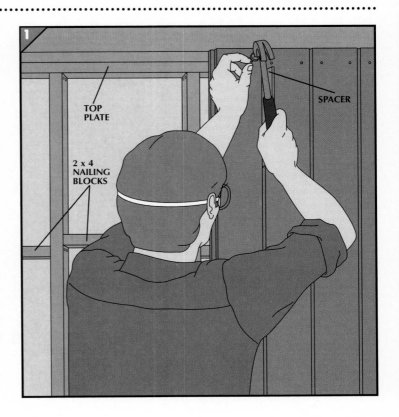

2. Keeping the boards vertical.

◆ Every six boards, fasten the top of the board with only one nail, then hold a level in the rabbet near the bottom of the board. Swing the board from side to side until it is plumb, then nail the board to the sole plate, the top plate, and the 2-by-4 blocks (above).

◆ At the end of the wall, install the first board of the adjacent wall as described in Step 1, if you plan to install paneling on the other side of the corner.

◆ Measure, mark, and cut the last board so it will fit snugly into the rabbet of the first board—or against the wall, if you are not paneling the adjacent wall—then nail it in place.

FITTING AND NAILING TONGUE-AND-GROOVE JOINTS

1. Driving the boards together.

◆ Align the first board against the corner, with the tongue facing out; plumb the board with a carpenter's level and nail through its face into the top and sole plates and into horizontal blocks as for rabbeted panels *(page 119)*.

◆ Slide the groove of the next board onto the tongue of the first and place a $\frac{1}{8}$-inch spacer between the two.

◆ Fit the groove of a hammering block—a short scrap of tongue-and-groove board—over the tongue of the new board near one end and strike the block firmly, driving the new board against the spacer block and the first board *(right)*. Slide the block along the length of the board, shifting the spacer accordingly as you work to the bottom of the board.

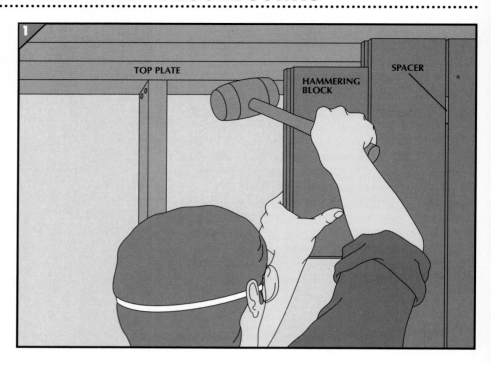

2. Nailing the tongue.

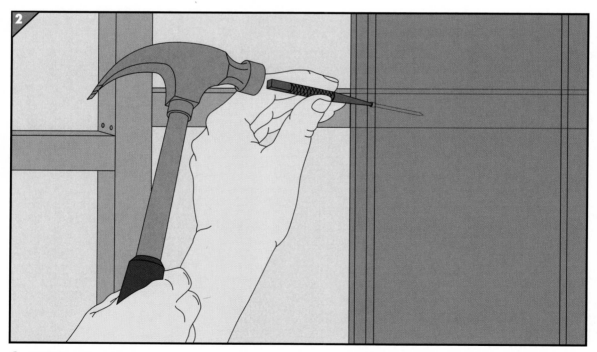

◆ Drive nails at a 45-degree angle partway through the base of the tongue, where it meets the body of the board, into the framing members behind the board *(above)*.

◆ Sink the nails with a nail set, taking care not to splinter the tongue. If a board is more than 8 inches wide, also nail it through its middle.

◆ Plumb every sixth board as you would a rabbeted one *(page 119, Step 2)*.

◆ At the end of the wall, cut off the tongue edge of the next-to-last board and install it by nailing through its face.

◆ Measure and mark the last board on the tongue edge so it will butt against the wall, cut it along the mark, and nail it with its groove against the cut edge of the next-to-last board.

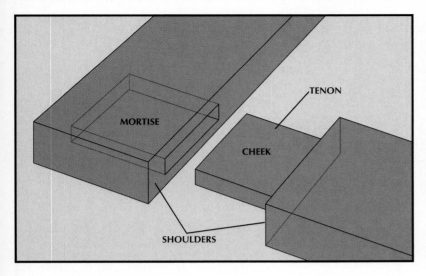

Anatomy of a blind mortise and tenon.
The mortise part of the joint has a width equal to one-third the thickness of the stock and a depth equal to three-quarters of the stock width. The projecting tenon is $\frac{1}{8}$ inch shorter than the depth of the mortise to allow space for glue. The sides of the tenon, called cheeks, fit snugly between the wide inner faces of the mortise, taking advantage of the strength achieved when the long grain of two pieces of wood is glued together. The shoulders of the mortise and tenon, on the bodies of the boards, fit together flush on all sides.

1. Setting the mortise gauge.
◆ Set a mortise chisel whose width is one-third to one-half the thickness of the wood to be joined on a workbench with the tip overhanging the edge of the bench.
◆ Loosen the thumbscrew on the fence of a mortise gauge, hold the gauge pins against the chisel tip, and set the gap between the pins equal to the chisel-tip width by turning the adjustment thumbscrew at the end of the bar *(right)*. If you are using a drill-press mortising attachment *(page 61)*, set the gauge to the width of its chisel.
◆ Hold the gauge against the edge of the board to be mortised, slide the bar through the fence until the pins are centered on the stock, and tighten the fence thumbscrew.

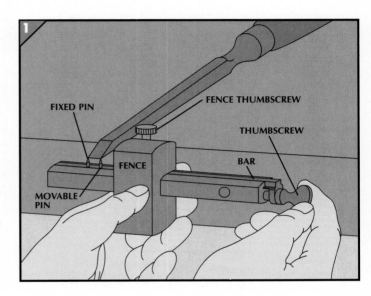

2. Marking the mortise.
◆ Clamp the board in a vise.
◆ Mark the ends of the mortise with a combination square and a utility knife.
◆ To outline the sides of the mortise, butt the fence of the mortise gauge against the workpiece and slide the tool along the stock.
◆ Score a line across the center of the outline with a utility knife and a combination square, then score lines $\frac{1}{8}$ inch to each side. Continue working toward the ends of the mortise, scoring lines at $\frac{3}{8}$-inch intervals, with the last lines about $\frac{1}{8}$ inch from each end *(left)*.

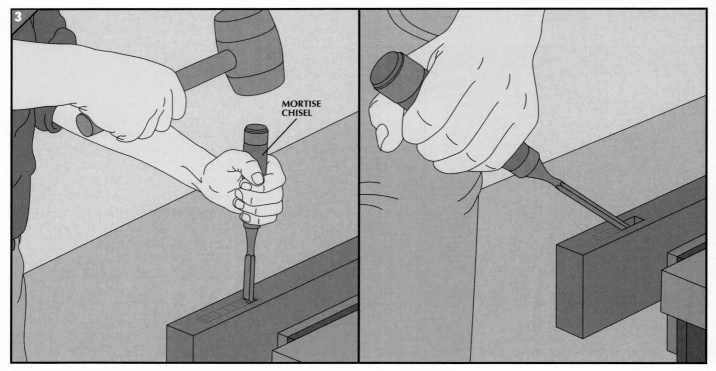

MORTISE
CHISEL

3. Chopping out the mortise.

◆ Starting at the scored line that is $\frac{1}{8}$ inch from one end of the mortise outline, hold the mortise chisel vertically with the bevel facing the waste, and strike the tool with a wooden mallet, making a cut about $\frac{1}{4}$ inch deep. Repeat the action at the next scored line *(above, left)*.

◆ Tilt the handle down toward the uncut portion of the outline so the tip of the blade digs in under the waste wood and severs it free *(above, right)*.

◆ Continue making cuts on every scored line and levering out the waste until you reach the line $\frac{1}{8}$ inch from the other end of the mortise. Then, turn the chisel around so the bevel faces in the opposite direction. Make a cut and lever out the waste.

◆ Repeat this process, chopping down and levering out the waste, until you reach the desired depth of the mortise.

◆ Trim the ends of the mortise by holding the chisel vertically, bevel facing the waste, and paring away the $\frac{1}{8}$-inch-wide waste sections at each end.

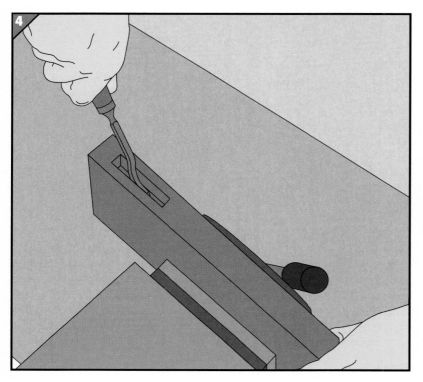

4. Smoothing the bottom of the cavity.

◆ Hold a lock mortise chisel—also called a swan-neck chisel—the same width as the mortise so the rounded back face of the blade is against one end of the mortise. Push the tool toward the other end *(left)*, smoothing the bottom of the mortise.

◆ Repeat the action, working from the opposite end.

CUTTING A TENON

1. Outlining the tenon.

◆ With a combination square and a utility knife, score shoulder lines across the faces and edge of the board at a distance from the end equal to the depth of the mortise less $\frac{1}{8}$ inch.

◆ With a mortise gauge *(page 121)*, score two parallel lines, called tenon lines, on the end of the board as far apart as the width of the mortise; extend the tenon lines along the edges of the board to meet the shoulder lines *(right)*.

◆ Score two lines with a utility knife across the end of the board, perpendicular to the scored tenon lines, to mark off the length of the tenon *(dashed lines)*. Then extend the lines down both faces of the board as far as the shoulder line.

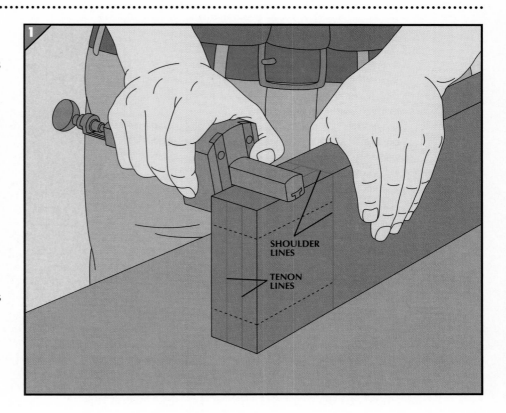

SHOULDER LINES

TENON LINES

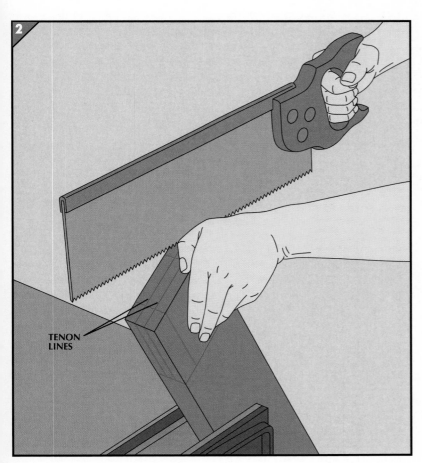

TENON LINES

2. Starting the tenon-line cuts.

◆ Secure the board at about a 60-degree angle in a vise, hold a backsaw at a 45-degree angle to the edge of the board, and saw along the waste side of each tenon line *(left)* until the kerf reaches the shoulder line.

◆ Turn the board over and cut the tenon lines on the other edge in the same way.

3. Completing the tenon-line cuts.

◆ Secure the board vertically in the vise.
◆ Set the saw in the kerfs of each tenon line and, keeping the blade horizontal, saw down to the shoulder lines *(right)*.
◆ Set the saw across each end of the board on the lines that mark the ends of the tenon and saw down to the shoulder lines.

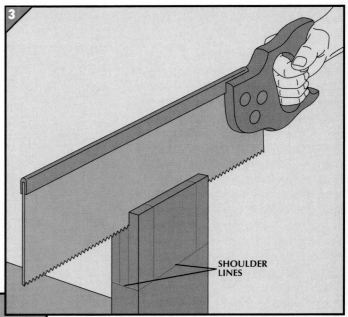

SHOULDER LINES

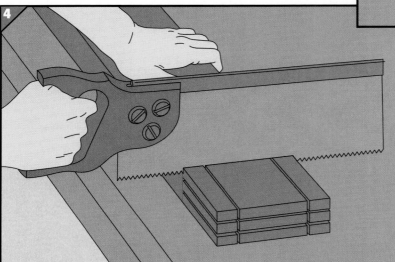

4. Cutting the shoulder lines.

◆ Set the board flat on a workbench and cut straight down along a shoulder line on the face until it meets a tenon cut *(left)*. Turn the board over and saw the second shoulder.
◆ Set the board on edge and saw from the shoulder line to the tenon, creating the third shoulder. Then place the board on its opposite edge and saw to the tenon to form the fourth shoulder.

5. Finishing the corners.

Grasp the blade of a bevel-edge chisel near the handle, place the flat side of the blade against the shoulder, and set the cutting edge in the corner where the shoulder and tenon meet. Raise one corner of the blade by tilting the handle away from you and slowly draw the chisel toward you to scrape any wood out of the shoulder-tenon corner. Keep your fingers out of the path of the blade—this is a rare instance when you must chisel toward, rather than away from, you.

Some woodworkers also use a skew chisel *(photograph)* to trim surfaces. Its angled cutting edge is well suited to shearing end grain and paring wood in corners.

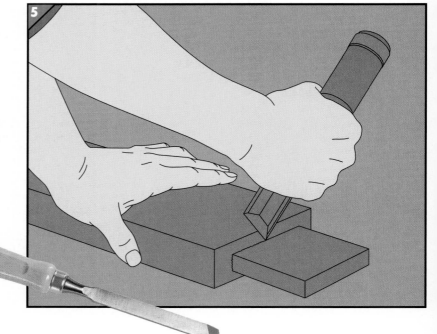

1. Test-fitting the joint.
◆ Clamp the mortised board horizontally in a vise and push the tenon in the mortise *(left)*, tapping it gently with a mallet if necessary.
◆ If you meet strong resistance, pull the tenon out and look for shiny spots on its cheeks—signs of bulges in the mortise or tenon. Pare away the shiny spots with a bevel-edge chisel or a skew chisel *(opposite, photograph)*, working across the grain with the bevel facing up. Test the fit again and pare the tenon until you can work it into the mortise, then separate the pieces.

If the tenon is loose in the mortise, glue and clamp a thin layer of wood to one or both cheeks, let the glue dry, and test the fit again.

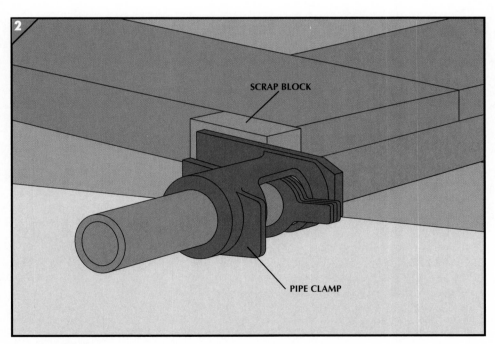

SCRAP BLOCK

PIPE CLAMP

2. Assembling the joint.
◆ With a finger, spread a thin layer of glue on the tenon; inside the mortise, use a thin scrap of wood to spread the glue.
◆ Slide the tenon into the mortise and set the pieces flat on a workbench.
◆ Hold the boards together with a long pipe clamp, protecting the stock with scrap blocks. Check the joint with a carpenter's square, then tighten the clamp *(above)*.

INDEX

TIME® LIFE BOOKS

Time-Life Books is a division of Time Life Inc.

TIME LIFE INC.
PRESIDENT and CEO: George Artandi

TIME-LIFE BOOKS
PRESIDENT: Stephen R. Frary
PUBLISHER/MANAGING EDITOR: Neil Kagan

HOME REPAIR AND IMPROVEMENT: Working with Wood
EDITOR: Lee Hassig
MARKETING DIRECTOR: James Gillespie
Art Directors: Kathleen Mallow, Barbara M. Sheppard
Associate Editor/Research and Writing: Karen Sweet
Marketing Manager: Wells Spence

Director of Finance: Christopher Hearing
Director of Book Production: Marjann Caldwell
Director of Operations: Eileen Bradley
Director of Photography and Research: John Conrad Weiser
Director of Editorial Administration: Barbara Levitt
Production Manager: Marlene Zack
Quality Assurance Manager: James King
Library: Louise D. Forstall

ST. REMY MULTIMEDIA INC.
President and Chief Executive Officer: Fernand Lecoq
President and Chief Operating Officer: Pierre Léveillé
Vice President, Finance: Natalie Watanabe
Managing Editor: Carolyn Jackson
Managing Art Director: Diane Denoncourt
Production Manager: Michelle Turbide

Staff for *Working with Wood*

Series Editors: Marc Cassini, Heather Mills
Art Director: Robert Paquet
Assistant Editor: John Dowling
Writer: Pierre Home-Douglas
Designers: Jean-Guy Doiron, Robert Labelle
Editorial Assistant: James Piecowye
Coordinator: Dominique Gagné
Copy Editor: Judy Yelon
Indexer: Linda Cardella Cournoyer
Systems Coordinator: Éric Beaulieu
Technical Support: Jean Sirois
Other Staff: Linda Castle, Lorraine Doré, Geneviève Dubé, Anne-Marie Lemay

PICTURE CREDITS
Cover: Photograph, Robert Chartier. Art, Maryo Proulx.

Illustrators: Jack Arthur, Gilles Beauchemin, Frederic F. Bigio from B-C Graphics, François Daxhelet, Roger C. Essley, Gerry Gallagher, Adsai Hemintranont, Walter Hilmers Jr., Fred Holz, Dick Lee, James Robert Long, John Massey, Peter McGinn, Joan S. McGurren, Bill McWilliams, Eduino Pereira, Jacques Perrault, Ray Skibinski, Whitman Studio Inc.

Photographers: **End papers:** Glenn Moores and Chantal Lamarre. **23, 44, 45, 47, 50, 53, 55, 76, 86, 90, 91, 102, 124:** Glenn Moores and Chantal Lamarre. **27:** Robert Chartier. **71 (upper):** DeWalt Industrial Tool Company Inc. **71 (lower):** Delta International Machinery Corp. **79:** Black & Decker Canada Inc. **96:** Senco Products Inc.

ACKNOWLEDGMENTS
The editors wish to thank the following individuals and institutions: Black & Decker Canada Inc., Richmond Hill, Ont.; Delta International Machinery Corp., Guelph, Ont.; DeWalt Industrial Tool Company Inc., Richmond Hill, Ont.; Louis V. Genuario, Genuario Construction Company Inc., Alexandria, VA; Hillman Fastener, Cincinnati, OH; Northwestern Steel and Wire Company, Sterling, IL; Senco Products Inc., Cincinnati, OH; Simpson Strong-Tie Company Inc., Pleasanton, CA; Stanley Tools, Division of Stanley Canada Inc., Burlington, Ont.

©1997 Time-Life Books. All rights reserved. No part of this book may be reproduced in any form or by any electronic or mechanical means, including information storage and retrieval devices or systems, without prior written permission from the publisher, except that brief passages may be quoted for reviews. First printing. Printed in U.S.A. Published simultaneously in Canada. School and library distribution by Time-Life Education, P.O. Box 85026, Richmond, Virginia 23285-5026.

TIME-LIFE is a trademark of Time Warner Inc. U.S.A.

Library of Congress Cataloging-in-Publication Data
Working with Wood / by the editors of Time-Life Books.
p. cm. — (Home repair and improvement)
Includes index.
ISBN 0-7835-3911-8
1. Carpentry—Amateurs' manuals.
I. Time-Life Books. II. Series.
TH5606.T55   1997
694—dc21   97-16888